Table of Contents

To Believe, Belong, Grow, and Live in Christ

Youth Ministry Is Crucial

Youth today are hungry for ways to help them understand a world that is dramatically different from the experience of previous generations. Changing values, a climate of violence, and an overall decline in US educational achievement are just a few of the cultural issues that have a significant impact on the growth and development of our teenagers today.

Declining church membership has us studying and talking about the definition and demonstration of vital ministry. Youth must be a part of the conversation. There is no such thing as the "church of tomorrow" if we do not nurture and teach our teens and children to be faithful disciples and leaders today.

Living Out Our Vision

Each youth ministry program needs a clear vision with concrete goals and a strong theological and biblical base. We who help develop and publish resources for youth ministry have an overall vision of youth ministry that is in constant flux as our culture shifts, as we find new ways to do things, and as the identity of youth changes from one year to the next. But some things are constant and deserve our attention and energy all year long. These major emphases include believing, belonging, growing, and living in Jesus Christ.

The UMY PROGRAM ANNUAL helps you understand and apply this vision in the lives of youth by addressing crucial youth issues in seven categories: personal, family, school, social, public, church, and spiritual. Within these program issues, we help youth understand some of the principles and the skills they need to believe, belong, grow, and live in Jesus Christ.

We Are Called to Believe

Believing means to cultivate Christian values and beliefs so that an empowering and loving image of Christ imbues and undergirds our actions and motivations.

Each program is biblically based, even though it is issue-oriented. Sometimes the Scripture selections and their application are obvious; other times the principle and context, though important and relevant, need more examination to make the connection between faith and life.

We Are Called to Belong

Belonging means to provide an atmosphere of understanding, acceptance, nurture, care, and love. The "Family" and "Church" sections identify the church as a community of faith and an extended family for its youth. These sections will also help youth counteract the forces that divide or alienate persons or negate their sense of belonging.

We Are Called to Grow

Growing means to have and provide opportunities for competence and capability, to support cumulative efforts to take on new tasks, and to learn from failures and successes. The "Spiritual" section helps youth grow in their ability to make decisions, evaluate choices, and examine consequences from a theological standpoint.

We Are Called to Live

Living means to gain a greater sense of autonomy as well as interdependence, not to be smothered or ignored; but to be respected, empowered, and trusted to set reasonable and responsible personal boundaries. The "Personal," "Social," "Public," and "Family" sections examine who we are and who we can or will become, not only by the issue-oriented decisions we make but also through the lens of our faith.

How to Use the UMY PROGRAM ANNUAL

How to Use the UMY PROGRAM ANNUAL

Welcome to the brand-new, easy-to-use United Methodist youth fellowship resources! These thirty-two new programs, along with the events and mission ideas in the *UMY Mission and Event Annual*, provide an "at-your-fingertips" means of planning a super, fun-filled, and issue-oriented year with your youth fellowship group.

Fun and a Whole Lot More

The programs will hold your group's interest with interactive activities that stimulate thinking and open up the topic for investigation. In addition to the potentially transformational learning, the programs are also written so that youth can gain leadership experience.

Easy to Use

The UMY PROGRAM ANNUAL is designed to be easy on the eye and easy to prepare. In each program, the essential, step-by-step instructions for each activity in the program are provided in the wide column. The activities have up to three "main ingredients"—instructions, marked with ➠; questions, in the tinted box; Scriptures, identified by ✝; and for-your-information items such as case studies, set apart with *.

These eye-catching symbols let you know immediately what kind of teaching/leading step you're in at any moment. In addition, each step of the program topic gives a suggested time. Feel free to take more or less time as your unique situation requires.

But it's not enough just to give instructions; we want you to have solid information behind the life issues you are examining. The narrow column, "For Your Information," provides in short paragraphs general topical information, Scripture background and commentary, more detailed instructions, and other related news to help you give depth and meaning to each program.

For Multiple Age Levels and Group Sizes

In one volume, you have what you need to tailor the programs to the age level and size of your group. Each program has options that can be used by either a broadly graded group or by separate groups of older and younger youth. And by gearing the activities to either one small group or clusters of small groups, the activities will work with any number of teens.

Convenient Organization

The thirty-two programs fall under seven major headings:

* *Personal* programs deal with individual (although widely-held) concerns.

* *Church* programs center on issues dealing with the life of a local congregation and the church as an institution.

* *Social* programs deal with relational or group issues.

* *Spiritual* programs look at faith development and theological concerns.

* *Public* programs address issues of the community, nation, or world.

* *Family* programs take a look at the family and its dynamics, including "traditional" and "non-traditional" family configurations.

* *School* programs relate to life at school, both in class and in extracurricular activities.

By organizing the programs this way, you will see, at a glance, what the core issue is for each program. You can select a whole year's worth of topics, picking and choosing what is most relevant and timely for your own group.

So, What D'ya Think?

Whether you are a long-time friend or a new friend of our youth fellowship resources, we hope you will find the UMY PROGRAM ANNUAL and its partner resource the *UMY Mission and Event Annual* to be just what you need for a Spirit-filled, vital youth ministry. Your comments and suggestions are welcome. Look on the inside front cover in the teeny tiny print for our address, or call Curric-U-Phone (800-251-8591). Write to or call the editor and we'll have a good conversation.

PLAN AND EXPECT SUCCESS!

United Methodists believe in ministry for, by, and with youth. We also believe great youth ministry can **reach** new youth and **connect** them with Jesus Christ and faithful friends. We can **nurture** youth as growing, vital disciples, and **send** youth into their community and world to witness to their faith through their attitudes and actions.

Some practical tips for sharing leadership and encouraging involvement include

* **WORK AS A TEAM**. From initial envisioning through evaluation, think and make decisions as a team of adults and youth.

* **FOCUS ON YOUR PURPOSE**. Insure that *everyone* knows the purpose of the program and why it's important.

* **SHARE RESPONSIBILITIES**. Involvement is a high priority. All the members of a group like to succeed and feel that they have made a difference by contributing in ways they are prepared to do well.

* **ENCOURAGE CREATIVITY**. Try new things. Monitor any attitudes or quick reflex responses that say "We can't do *that*!"

* **ANTICIPATE RESULTS**. Continually discuss what you expect to happen as a result of this program.

A SUCCESSFUL PROGRAM

Life-changing, challenging youth programs are the result of prayer, planning, preparation, and participation. Here is a time line that will help the planning team feel confident as they meet to develop program plans.

Three Weeks Prior to the Program
* Review UMY PROGRAM ANNUAL materials and options.
* Share initial ideas and possibilities.
* Identify next week's agenda for planning.

Two Weeks Prior to the Program
* Complete working Planner Sheet.
* Identify what parts need to be improved.
* Designate who's responsible for any necessary improvements.

One Week Prior to the Program
* Review final Planner Sheet.
* Walk through the program.

One Hour Prior to the Program
* Have a final walk-through of program.
* Have a brief time of prayer together.

DESIGN FOR PROGRAMS

Effective youth ministry programs include creativity, variety, high energy, and full participation by the youth and adults of the youth group. Every program should include each of these elements, though they will vary in length, emphasis, and style depending on the focus of the program.

* **WELCOME AND GATHERING TIME.** Welcoming persons is crucial. Welcoming can be done informally or in a way that ties in with the purpose of the program. Nametags help build overall familiarity and can also fit the program theme. This is a terrific time to take attendance and care for details, such as registrations for upcoming events or projects. Some lively background music adds to the atmosphere!

* **ICEBREAKERS.** This time may include games, songs, homemade videos, or other ways to bring persons together in non-threatening ways to ease everyone into making new friends and affirming ongoing friendships.

* **COMMUNITY BUILDING.** Well-chosen games, activities, simulations, or fun problem-solving puzzles can involve youth and adults in having fun and getting to know one another at a deeper level. These activities call for more personal sharing, but should not make anyone feel uncomfortable.

* **PROGRAM.** The main portion of the program is presented through a carefully chosen and designed sequence of activities. Allow time for reflection, conversation, and evaluation. Each program in the UMY PROGRAM ANNUAL will last for about forty minutes.

* **CLOSING DEVOTIONAL MOMENTS.** Well-designed worship, reflecting the purpose of the program, allows youth and adults to assess the meaning of the program and strengthens their relationships with one another, with the church, and with Christ.

• •

UMYF PROGRAM PLANNER

PROGRAM TITLE_____ PROGRAM DATE_____

PLANNING TEAM MEMBERS:

PROGRAM PURPOSE:

GOALS:
  1.

  2.

  3.

FOCUS: THIS PROGRAM IS IMPORTANT BECAUSE

CRITERIA FOR SUCCESS: WE WILL BE SUCCESSFUL IF

PLANNING CHART

Time Frame	Activity	Related Goals	Leader(s)	Supplies	Evaluation

Note: Local churches may photocopy this page without securing permission.

More Power for Your Youth Programming

NEW! UMY MISSION AND EVENT ANNUAL:
Workshops, Retreats, & Mission Ideas for Youth.

◆ **For youth grades 7–12 and adult workers with youth**
◆ **Published annually; updated**
◆ **UM approved resource**
◆ **UM specific content**
◆ **Basic resource: Mission and Event Annual**

Successfully plan longer programs of interest and reach youth through consideration of issues important to them! *UMY Mission and Event Annual* provides eight events that can be used as retreats, successive workshops, or all-day programs. Selected events include: "Youth Ministry: Believing, Belonging, Growing, and Living in Christ"; "What's All This Psychic Stuff?"; "Sexual Harassment in School"; and "Boy Versus Girl: I Don't Understand You."

UMY Mission and Event Annual also offers great ideas for engaging teens in missions with a concise, fifteen-page "Mission How-To" section. Youth leaders will have plenty of help planning how to be in mission—in another locale or in their own backyard. Programs include: "Hunger in the U.S.A.," "Homelessness in America," "and Migrant Families."
#780853. **$9.95**

NEW! MUDPIE OLYMPICS AND 99 OTHER NONEDIBLE GAMES

◆ **For youth grades 7–12 and adult workers with youth**
◆ **Updated**
◆ **UM approved resource**
◆ **Basic resource: Game Book**

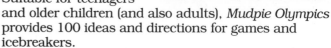

Have a field day of fun with *Mudpie Olympics and 99 Other Nonedible Games!* Suitable for teenagers and older children (and also adults), *Mudpie Olympics* provides 100 ideas and directions for games and icebreakers.

Downplaying the competitive aspects of games, these activities stress cooperation, interdependence, and interaction. For instance, *Mudpie Olympics* suggests ways to divide teams arbitrarily, avoiding any feelings of being the "odd person out."

Games are aligned by category: big events, relays, group building or bonding activities, get-acquainted games, active indoor or outdoor games, and communication games.
#780950. **$9.95**

PERSONAL ISSUES

PERSONAL

Shooting for Shoes

by Natalie L. Woods

PURPOSE:

To help youth cope with violent theft of their clothing or other personal property, focusing on recognizing and avoiding dangerous situations as well as what to do and how to seek protection if they or someone they know is threatened.

PREPARATION

➡ Gather several newspapers and one pair of scissors for each small group.
➡ Obtain balloons in several colors for the **I Want It!** game.
➡ Provide Bibles and commentaries.
➡ Have *Youth! Praise* and a cassette/CD player handy for the worship segment.

FOR YOUR INFORMATION

GUN ACCESSIBILITY FOR TEENS

Nearly six out of ten students in the sixth through twelfth grades "could get a gun if they wanted one" reports LH Research who conducted this 1993 national survey in April and May for the Chicago-based Joyce Foundation. Nearly four out of ten students claim to know personally someone who has been injured or killed by gunfire.

Of the 2,508 students surveyed, fifteen percent claim to have carried a handgun in the month prior to the survey. Four percent had carried a gun to school. These students attend public, private, and Catholic schools in the suburbs, farm towns, and inner cities.

Other statistics: Nine percent

I WANT IT! (15 minutes)

➡ This game works best in a building with several rooms with each team having a "safety zone" room.

➡ Form two or more teams and give each team an equal number of balloons: at least three balloons per group member. Have volunteers randomly place balloons throughout the building.

➡ Give each team the following instructions:

* Each team has assigned colors and must retrieve their color balloons and take them to their safety zone.
* Players may (but do not have to) pop the other team's balloons, but may not use their hands.
* Players may enter only their own safety zones.
* The team with the most rescued balloons wins.

➡ Gather the teams together after the game and discuss the following questions:

> Did the focus of the activity become "rescuing" your balloons at any cost? If so, when?
> What was your attitude about your opponents' balloons? Why?

Do movies, TV programs, and/or popular music (audio or video) support the notion that "possession is nine tenths of the law"? that "doing whatever it takes" is okay to get what you want? If so, how?

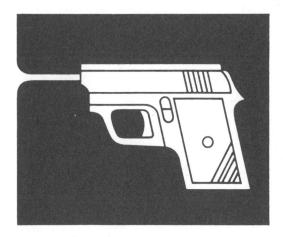

THE "ME" MENTALITY (10 minutes)

➦ Form small groups of three to five persons and give each group a stack of newspapers and a pair of scissors.

➦ Ask the participants to search first for incidents of violent theft (carjacking, armed burglary, student thefts at school, and so on), and then for articles dealing with trials or sentencing of people who have committed such crimes. Focus on the accused's reasons for committing the crime. (See FYI: "Gun Accessibility for Teens" and "Ending the Violence in Schools.")

➦ Have each small group list the reasons given for such crimes.

➦ Then ask these questions:

Why would someone hurt or kill another person for a pair of shoes or a jacket?
Do you think these people place a low value on human life? Why, or why not?
Is terrorism a way of life in school? on the street? in the home?
What are some causes of violent theft?
What are some items that are "at risk" for theft during school hours?
Is it worth the risk to wear or to own these items? Why, or why not?

have shot at someone; eleven percent have been fired at; thirty-eight percent acknowledge that the threat of violence has changed where they hang out, their friends, and their activities; thirty-five percent believe it's highly likely they will be "cut down" by gunfire; twenty-five percent say "something would be missing without guns"; fifty-five percent agree with the use of metal detectors in schools; only seven percent said their schools use metal detectors.
(Adapted from *The Dallas Morning News*, July 20, 1993.)

ENDING THE VIOLENCE IN SCHOOLS

What can be done to end the violence in schools? It must begin with changing our attitudes toward violence.

Requiring students to pass through metal detectors is a start. Some schools have uniformed police and guards patrolling the halls. Other schools ban lockers and book bags. More critical areas have bullet drills to train students to dive for cover when gunfire is heard.

Students need to discuss violence because it involves issues of justice, fear, equity, and power. Some schools have instituted weekly conflict-resolution programs. Gun-safety awareness programs have increased.

The Center to Prevent Handgun Violence in Washington, DC, offers a comprehensive curriculum called Straight Talk About Risks (STAR) that teaches kids how to stay safe if they see a gun, how to resist peer pressure to carry guns, and how to differentiate between television and the real world.

Deborah Prothrow-Stith, M.D., assistant dean of the Harvard School of Public Health and the author of *Deadly Consequences*, developed a ten-session course titled "Violence Prevention Curriculum for Adolescents" that teaches conflict resolution and helps alert students to the risks.

Last, but not least, the National PTA recommends that each school develop guidelines for discipline, safety, and crisis intervention.

SCRIPTURE (20 minutes)

These Scriptures serve to help teens understand the biblical perspective on possessions, violence, and dealing with others.

➡ Divide into age-level groups and assign the following Scriptures to each group. Provide commentaries.

✞ **Exodus 20:13, 15, 17** (three commandments)
✞ **Psalm 71:1-6** (asking for God's care)
✞ **Matthew 6:19-24** (No one shall serve two masters.)
✞ **Matthew 6:25-34** ("What shall we wear?")

Older Youth

➡ Form small groups and read, research, and discuss insights and learnings from the Scriptures. Discuss them with the whole age-level group.

➡ Then discuss the following questions:

What role does God and/or faith play in your life as it concerns possessions? violence and safety?

How can you use these Scriptures to help you keep ownership in its proper perspective? to avoid potentially violent acts?

As Christians, how should we relate to the victim of a crime of covetousness? to the perpetrator?

Who do you go to when dealing with a potentially violent situation?

Younger Youth

➡ In small discussion groups of four, read the passages, study the commentary, talk about what they mean, and choose one or more to put in the form of a modern parable.

➡ Present the modern-day parable to the entire group.

➡ Then discuss the following questions:

What are the purposes of possessions or material goods according to these Scriptures?

What do these Scriptures tell us about having and desiring possessions? about God's care and provision for us?

What are the purposes of clothing according to your peers and the media?

Are you ever concerned about the clothes/shoes you wear? Why, or why not?

Are you ever jealous of the clothes/shoes that your peers wear? When? Why?

DEFUSING A CHARGED SITUATION (20 minutes)

➡ Have two or three volunteers act out one of the "charged scenarios."(See FYI.)

➡ Each situation should be acted out twice. The first time will demonstrate a violent conclusion. The second time will recognize the language and/or actions of potential violence and avoid, cope with, or deter a possibly violent conclusion.

➡ After all the dramas, ask these questions:

> How can some of these types of situations be avoided?
>
> What are some of your fears and feelings concerning personal theft and violence?
>
> Why are certain name-brand shoes and clothing important enough to youth for another youth to steal (and kill) in order to have them?
>
> What does **Psalm 71:1-6** tell us about justice and God's care?

CHARGED SCENARIOS

1. It's 12:30 A.M. and you are walking home with friends from another friend's house wearing your new name-brand sneakers and matching designer outfit. A car pulls up in front of you with three teens demanding your clothes and shoes. They have weapons.

2. You've just celebrated your birthday and have received that very special piece of jewelry you've been wanting. You wore it to school today and during lunch it was not only snatched from you, but you suffered cuts and bruises.

3. You and your best friend wear your matching jackets (the latest fashion trendsetter and not cheap by any means) to the game Friday night. You and your friend leave the game early. Later that evening, you awake in the hospital to learn that your jackets are gone and your friend is critically injured.

WORSHIP

Paraphrase Psalm 23. Using newsprint and a marker, write down contemporary words and images. Relate the psalm to God's presence, help, and comfort in dealing with violent theft of name-brand shoes, and so on.

Sing "Jesus Loves Me, Mon" from *Youth! Praise.*

Read the Scriptures starting with the paraphrase of the psalm and then **Matthew 6:19-24.**

Close with a circle prayer based on the premise that your heart is where your treasure is. Invite participants to complete the sentence "Lord, my Banker and my Protector, my heart lies with . . ."

The Ups and Downs of Dating

by Natalie L. Woods

PURPOSE:

To help youth sort through their feelings about dating and their dating patterns and examine the on-again/off-again nature of teen male-female relationships, how this pattern helps develop social skills, and some of the different needs and expectations of males and females in social relationships.

PREPARATION

➡ Provide newsprint and markers, tape, paper, and pencils for each person.
➡ Have on hand Bibles, copies of *The United Methodist Hymnal*, and at least one commentary on First Corinthians.

FOR YOUR INFORMATION

WHY DATE?

1. To grow socially, emotionally, and spiritually. A dating relationship provides the opportunity to develop skills in social relationships and communication with one another, including being able to talk about how we really feel. Have you ever considered that your dating relationship will help you to grow either closer to God (from a greater desire to pray, the need to experience the Word, and sharing Christ with your date) or away from God?

2. To help fulfill the basic human need to love and to be loved. This falls right next to the need for food and water. Dating is one of the ways you can learn to give and to receive love in healthy ways.

WHY DATE? (10 minutes)

➡ Review some of the reasons for dating. (See FYI.) Use these reasons and the reflection questions they include in the following activity.

Older Youth

➡ In small groups of four, talk about the reasons for dating and the advantages and disadvantages of dating.

➡ Have a spokesperson from each group share with the other groups at least three of those reasons. Then talk about the following questions:

From your group's consensus, which is more advantageous: To date or not to date? Why, or why not?
Do you know "who you are"? **and** "who you are in a relationship with someone else"?
Do you need someone to be whole? Why, or why not?
What do you expect from your girlfriend/boyfriend relationship?
How much will you put up with to keep a relationship? What's fair? What's healthy for you? What's healthy for both of you?

Younger Youth

➠ Brainstorm some reasons for dating.

➠ Write these reasons on newsprint with a marker. Then discuss these questions:

> What are some advantages of dating?
> What are some disadvantages (problems) of dating?
> What does it mean to "know who I am"? Is it important to know? Give reasons for your answer.
> If so, then who am I in a relationship with someone else?
> Am I okay if I don't feel like dating right now?
> Socially, how am I different from the opposite sex right now?

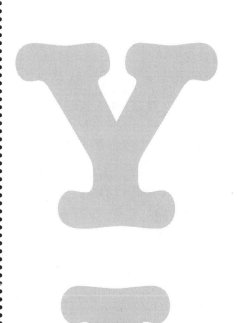

MALE/FEMALE SENSITIVITY (15 minutes)

Many people enter into relationships having no idea or understanding of the needs or wants of members of the opposite sex.

➠ Read aloud **1 Corinthians 7:1-9, 32-38** — Paul's advice concerning marriage. (See FYI.)

➠ From your own impressions, respond to the statements on page 14. (Y is yes, M is maybe, and N is no.)

3. To have a good time and to relax. Aside from the spiritual benefits of dating, dating is a great way just to have a good time with someone you care about.

4. To help identify qualities of your future mate and provide a pool of potential marriage partners. As you date, you are subconsciously deciding what you want in your future companion (dependability, compassion, humor, and so on).

CONCERNING MARRIAGE

In **1 Corinthians 7:1-9, 32-38**, Paul is responding to a letter from the Corinthians concerning marriage and other points of interest. Paul's *personal* opinion was that celibacy was the best way of life for persons awaiting the second coming of the Lord, which Paul thought was imminent. He assumed that marriage was a primary distraction from *the affairs of the Lord*.

Paul is not against the institution of marriage and does not advise abstinence within a marriage. Paul recognizes the strength of the sex instinct and advises that "it is better to marry than to be aflame with passion" **(1 Corinthians 7:9)**.

LIVING THROUGH BREAKUPS

The down side of teenage dating, especially those relationships of any duration, is that of breaking up, even though it is a natural part of the process of dating and growing up. One of the most painful times in any young person's life is immediately following a serious breakup. Bad breakups can cause emotional, spiritual, or even physical damage to one or both people involved. But breakups are learning experiences and do not have to cause severe damage.

* Before making important decisions, go to a friend whom you trust and respect, explaining the situation and asking for advice. Think about what you are doing, what you like and don't like, and what your motivation is for staying or not staying in a relationship.

* If you are dissatisfied with the relationship, don't hide that fact. Let the other person know that things aren't okay with you. Do this with respect.

* Be honest and (although it may hurt) tell the person **why** you want to break up. Do this with respect too. Watch out for the temptation to wound.

* Mention positive things about the person and/or the relationship in a supportive way as you break up.

➠ About midway through, have the group members remind one another of the Cinderella and Sleeping Beauty fairy tales.

Y M N Men and women are created to be in partnership and companionship with one another.
Y M N Remaining single is an option.
Y M N Couples should live in mutual respect and love.
Y M N Spirituality has no part in a relationship.
Y M N A relationship that ends in a breakup can prepare us for other relationships.
Y M N God has given us all the same gifts.
Y M N Paul, the writer of the Letters to the Corinthians, feels that one should keep his or her desire under control.
Y M N This Scripture has nothing to do with teenage dating.
Y M N It is okay for me to ask questions about what is fair or what is healthy for me in my relationships.
Y M N I expect my prince/princess to know exactly what I want without my having to voice it.
Y M N I expect to live "happily ever after" when the right person comes along.
Y M N I expect love to overcome all obstacles, including any bad or annoying habits my special friend may have or I may have.

BREAKING UP IS HARD TO DO—AND LIVE THROUGH
(25 minutes)

➠ Introduce this activity with information about living through breakups. (See FYI.)

➠ Looking at the reactions on page 15, discuss (or perform skits on) breaking up and how a person is affected from a mild to an extreme degree of feelings.

➠ Deal with the breakup from both points of view: the person initiating the breakup and the person who is being dropped.

➡ After the discussion or skits, divide into age-level groups for a discussion of the questions that follow.

Self-Image
Intact...Damaged

Depression
Minimal..Intense

Loneliness
Being alone..Being lonely

Bitterness
Hurt..Anger

Mistrust of Opposite Sex
One person...All of them

Physical Problems
Headache..Chronic Illness

Poor "Witness" to Others
Caring concern ....Callous unconcern

Older Youth

How is breaking up like someone dying? (Psychologically, we must deal with the grieving process: denial, anger, guilt, grief, acceptance.)

What are some practical ways you can respond to a breakup? (Talk it over with a friend, beware of rebounding too quickly with a new relationship, avoid seeing the old boyfriend/girlfriend too much, stay busy, learn to turn to God and to trust God with the hurts in our lives.)

Younger Youth

What do you compare breaking up with?

Are there some "right ways" or "right times" to break up? What are they?

* Once the decision to break up has been made, don't back out. Putting it off or having to do it again only makes it harder for both people involved.

* Pray for the person you break up with to get over the hurt quickly and without serious emotional, physical, or spiritual problems.

WORSHIP

Each person will need a sheet of paper and a pencil. Have the participants write their name at the top of their paper. Tape all the sheets of paper on the walls.

Gather in a circle. Give the writing supplies to everyone.

Affirm one another's gifts. Have youth write on each paper a biblical and social dating quality (make it positive) that each person possesses.

Close with a word circle prayer. "Lord, twenty years from now when my own child asks me about dating, I'll say . . ."

Sing "When Love Is Found" (No. 643 in *The United Methodist Hymnal*).

Who Defines My Identity?

by Natalie L. Woods

PURPOSE:

To help youth sort through the expectations that they place on themselves as well as the expectations that others—family, church, school, media—place on teens to act or be a particular way, identify expectations that are reasonable, and think through who they are.

PREPARATION

➠ Gather poster paper, construction paper, tape, scissors, Bibles, magazines, and photos illustrating influences in a young person's life.

➠ Become familiar enough with the life of Dr. Martin Luther King, Jr., to talk about how his faith in Christ led him to lead the civil rights movement of the 1960's.

➠ Obtain a candle, matches, and items to symbolize identity influences for worship.

➠ Have on hand a copy of *Youth! Praise 2* and a cassette/CD player.

FOR YOUR INFORMATION

BUILDING A HOUSE OF IDENTITY

On a piece of large poster paper, have each participant sketch the diagram of the floor plan of a house. In each room of the house will be a display of values, expectations, attitudes, and ideas that have come from particular areas including parents, brothers, sisters, grandparents, school friends, teachers, television and other media, church, or a pastor. There might also be a hidden room for things the participant likes to keep hidden in his or her life.

To create the display, the participants may use pictures taken from

---

THE HOUSE OF IDENTITY (15 minutes)

➠ Instruct participants to organize a "display of identity" to be used in guiding them to learn more about themselves and others. The display will be of "rooms in a house." (See FYI.)

➠ Divide participants into groups of five or six. Ask them to take turns giving guided tours of "my house" (my identity).

➠ Ask these questions:

What did you place in the most important rooms of your home?

How do these attitudes, values, and ideas affect the rest of your life?

What did you put in the hidden rooms of your house? Why?

What attitudes or expectations do you get from the church?

What place do these have in your life?

Which values and expectations seem reasonable to you? unreasonable?

16

TAKE A BIBLE TOUR (10 minutes)
Older Youth

You have constructed a personal house; now you will put together a biblical house. Obviously you will have to use some different categories from those used in the earlier personal display. Some categories that might be used for the following characters are brother, mother, father, riches, fame, glory, God's will, service for God, and so on.

➡ In small groups of four to six persons, ask the participants to read one of the following passages and construct from their imaginations and the Scripture how they believe these particular biblical characters might construct their "house" of identity.

✞ **Genesis 32:22-32** (Jacob and the angel)
✞ **1 Samuel 3:1-20** (Samuel in the Temple)
✞ **Jeremiah 1:4-10** (Jeremiah's call)
✞ **Matthew 4:1-11** (Jesus' temptation)

➡ Allow time for each small group to report on their display; then ask these questions:

> For each of these characters what are the attitudes and values placed in the most important places of the house?
>
> How do you see this in the Scripture passage?
>
> What might your life look like now if God were the central value for you?
>
> If you followed the biblical characters' examples, do you think you would be different? If so, how?

magazines or words and phrases representing expectations, attitudes, values, and ideas that have influenced them from each of these areas. For example, they may put the expectations, values, attitudes, and ideas gained from parents in the living room because they are the ones that feel most comfortable. These displays should reflect not only the expectations, values, attitudes, and formative ideas of youth but also their position of importance in their lives.

Note: The individual areas should be movable so that later choices can incorporated.

THE POWERBALL EXERCISE

Use a soft ball or small terry cloth towel tied in a knot. The person holding the powerball gives a response to the question and then throws the ball to someone else, who must attempt to answer. The idea is to respond and throw as quickly as possible.

DR. MARTIN LUTHER KING, JR.

The son of an ordained Baptist minister, Martin knew at an early age that he was going to be a preacher. He came from a very loving and strong family. As an African American person growing up in the American South in the 1940's, he saw his friends and family treated less than fairly by many white people in that day. African Americans of that day could not eat in the same restaurants, drink from the same water fountains, or use the same restrooms as white persons. King's friends and family had to ride in the back of the bus to make room for white persons in the front. They could not get good jobs because they were black.

From 1955 until his death in 1968, Dr. Martin Luther King, Jr., became the prophetic voice of peaceful, nonviolent Christ-centered protest against these civil rights injustices. He challenged Americans to judge one another not on the color of skin but on the content of character. Over the course of thirteen years he was beaten and put in jail many times. Although his life was threatened many times, he refused to seek his personal safety because of his strong belief in being obedient to God and his faith in Jesus. King will not be forgotten as one who lived his faith as Christ-centered.

Younger Youth

➡ Ask all the participants to read **Matthew 6:25-33** and to keep their Bibles open to the passage.

➡ Use a "powerball" method to call out and list the key words and phrases from the passage, such as "do not worry," "life is more than food," and so on. Paraphrasing is okay. (See FYI.)

➡ When the list is complete, look at the comparisons and comments Jesus has made. Then ask these questions:

What do the key words and phrases tell you about Jesus? about how God takes care of us?
To what did Jesus compare the lilies? the birds?
What questions did Jesus say were unnecessary?
Who will supply your needs?
What new things does this passage suggest for your "house"?
If you followed these directions, do you think you would be different? If so, how?

A CHRIST-CENTERED IDENTITY (5 minutes)

➡ Read or tell the story of Dr. Martin Luther King, Jr., or another figure who seems to have made Christ the center of his or her identity. (See FYI.) Then ask these questions:

What do you know about the influences in this person's life?
What do you think made him or her put Jesus' attitudes, values, and expectations first?
How did putting Jesus first affect the person's life?
How do you think "seeking his kingdom first" would change your life?

REARRANGING THE FURNITURE OF LIFE (15 minutes)

Earlier the group members identified values and expectations, considered which ones seemed reasonable and which ones did not, and examined several Scripture passages as well as at least one story of how a contemporary person identified with Christ.

➠ Ask the group members to spend a few moments in silent reflection to process the information and activities they have been exposed to so far.

➠ After a few moments ask the youth to go again to their display and to rearrange the "furniture" in their lives now, considering biblical and other influences.

➠ Gather in the same small groups formed during the initial "house tour" and talk briefly about what changes were made and why. Then talk about these questions:

> Do values or expectations that seemed unreasonable before seem any more reasonable now? Give your reasons.
> Who do you now think defines your identity? What do you think and feel about that influence? Why?

REARRANGING THE FURNITURE

Two other programs may help with establishing and negotiating expectations: "Does My Family Trust Me? Do I Trust Them?" beginning on page 108 and "Why Can't I? Setting Rules and Boundaries" beginning on page 112.

WORSHIP

Gather in a circle around a lighted candle. Arrange around the candle symbols representing influences on our identity: from parents, a special note or letter of encouragement; from school, a book or report card; from church, the Bible; and so on. Explain how these influences have been important in shaping who we are.

Name the good influences in your lives that have helped you become your "best selves." As each one names people or other influences, the group responds by praying together aloud, "We give you thanks, O God."

Name the poor influences that have directed you in ways that have been against God. As each person names at least one influence, the group responds in prayer by saying, "Have mercy on us, O God."

Name the new decisions you have made about how to rearrange or reinterpret the influences on your life. As each person names his or her decision, ask the group to respond in prayer by saying, "Give us strength, O God."

Close by singing "A Charge to Keep I Have" from *Youth! Praise 2.*

PERSONAL

Lower Than Dirt

by A. Okechukwu Ogbonnaya

▶ PURPOSE:

To help youth learn ways to cope with those times when someone (especially someone significant) treats them like dirt.

▶ PREPARATION

➡ Bring three small containers, plain paper, pencils or pens, several pieces of newsprint or poster paper, colored paper for a collage, scissors, and paper glue.

➡ Have a Bible and a copy of *Songs of Zion* for each person. Provide commentaries for First Peter, Genesis, and Hebrews.

➡ Thoroughly review the information about adolescence. (See FYI, pages 20–22.)

➡ *Optional:* Gather props for the news crew.

FOR YOUR INFORMATION

PSYCHOLOGICAL PERSPECTIVE

Adolescence is a relatively new phenomenon, an "invention" of the twentieth century, and is by definition a time of transition. At a time when teens are beginning to push and test the limits of childhood, many of their parents are entering a time of changing capabilities themselves. Teens are required to work through a transition with those who have already made the adolescent transition and who face another transition at midlife.

The unequal distribution of power between a parent and a child comes into view as teens begin to lobby for a greater share. These dynamics set the scene for conflict, which though not

A MIME ENCOUNTER SESSION (5-10 minutes)

➡ Ask for volunteers to silently act out certain ways in which one may be treated "like dirt." Form three groups of two persons each. The remaining group members should observe and take notes.

NEWS INTERVIEW (10 minutes)

➡ Form a "news crew" of three persons playing the parts of reporters. They will ask the "persons on the street" the following questions:

> Describe for me the way in which the members treated each other. What did you just see?
>
> Was anyone treated "like dirt"? If so, why do you think he or she was treated that way?
>
> What do you think of the way the persons were treated? Would you like to be treated that way? Why, or why not?
>
> How do you think it made the other person feel? How did it make you feel?
>
> What do you think the receiver of the treatment should do? What would you do?

THE FEELING TRIANGLE
(10 minutes)

➠ Distribute three pieces of paper and a pencil to each person.

➠ Without using names, members of the group should write down three positive character traits—ideas about themselves that allow them to affirm their self-worth. The papers should now be placed in a container.

➠ On the second paper, the participants will write a negative word they may say to someone they wanted to feel "like dirt." Place these in a second container.

➠ On the third piece of paper, members are to write one word or brief phrase denoting how to react to someone who treats them "like dirt." Place these papers in the third container.

➠ Shake each container to mix up the papers. Place the containers where everyone in the group can see them. Now have each member choose a piece of paper from each container. Each member should have three pieces of paper.

➠ Ask the participants to read aloud the content of the papers in sequence: positive, negative, reaction. Each reader can describe his or her feelings and state whether he or she agrees or disagrees with the reaction.

SCRIPTURE TIME: (10-15 minutes)

Older Youth

➠ Form two teams. Assign **1 Peter 1:22-23** to one and **2:9-12** to the other. Provide commentaries. Each team needs a recorder to jot down answers to the questions for the specific passage after they have done some research.

1 Peter 1:22-23

How can the idea that you are born of an "imperishable seed" help you keep your self-value in the face of negative attacks?

What does verse 23 mean in terms of the way you feel and speak about yourself?

How can the concept of "the living and enduring word of God" help you ground your self-worth?

---

inevitable or constant, helps shape a teenager's sense of self and sense of autonomy.

Much energy and interest are invested in one's peers and the impact, even dominance, of the peer group is another critical influence on a teen's self-identity. Fitting in and getting along in peer interactions is as important as being able to exist independently. The crunch hits when a teen does not have the internal support of healthy self-esteem to weather the stormy spots of relational tensions and a new sense of autonomy.

Those youth who have dealt with the tensions should understand that their self-value, though connected to others, does not depend wholly on what others think of them.

OTHER CULTURES

In some cultures the issue of identity and autonomy is dealt with in adolescence by the process of initiation so that the prolonged period of childhood, which is common in the West, is avoided. This does not necessarily make for a smooth transition. But it does provide these possibilities: (1) The adolescent is no longer looked at and talked to as a "baby"; and (2) the initiation provides the adolescent with an opportunity to gain, through self-initiated activity, the right to adulthood.

YOUTH AND CLASS

Social and/or economic class needs to be considered as an important factor for determining a general self-concept within the bounds of one's general society. While the naming of the minority by the general society does not necessarily result in self-depreciation, it is true that societal definitions of persons affect their self-perception.

Within the United States it must be remembered that a prolonged childhood is a luxury only the majority can afford. Many minority children take on adult roles at an early age because of their place within the social system.

PEER GROUP

The importance of the peer group for the self-perception of youth cannot be overemphasized. The adolescent peer group may provide a new basis for trust that helps to determine the self-concept of a youth, particularly if the adolescent has developed a feeling of distrust for parents. In such cases "putdowns" by peers can have lasting effects on the behavioral orientation of a teen. On the other hand, encouraging and self-building words from peers can serve to enhance an adolescent's self-perception and help him or her react positively to various negations of the self by others.

Christian youth must remember that their peers' opinion of who they are must be considered in light of who they understand themselves to be in God.

1 Peter 2:9-12

What are the positive adjectives used to describe you as God's child? What does the passage say you are not?

What does the passage encourage you to do when faced with a negation of your self-worth?

For what things within this passage may one be moved legitimately to criticize a child of God?

➡ After the Scripture exploration, gather older youth together to make a collage of ideas. Distribute two pieces of colored paper to each participant.

➡ Persons from either group can mention ideas from their reading and research. Have the teens describe their idea on one of the pieces of colored paper; then, on a second piece of colored paper, have each teen create a drawing that depicts his or her understanding of the idea. Have everyone post his or her idea and its depiction on the wall. Form a collage of ideas and pictures.

Younger Youth

➡ Assign **Genesis 1:26-28** and **Hebrews 10:24-25**.

➡ Ask each individual to remember the group's response to one of the following questions:

Who is created in the image of God?

How do you think God sees you in relation to the Genesis passage? Why?

Do think that it is God's desire for us to put down one another? Give a reason for your answer.

What are some of the negative things we say to one another that make us feel bad?

According to the Hebrews passage, what are we to do with one another?

What are some ways we can help build the self-esteem of others?

➡ After reviewing the group members' answers, have them create a short song and/or dance reflecting their understanding of the issue.

PUTTING IT IN PRACTICE
(10-15 minutes)

➠ After the original roleplay and Scripture study, act out another scene to practice coping with being treated poorly. Mix younger and older youth as partners. Make up a scene or use one that follows. Debrief afterward.

* Jan's sister Gail never misses a chance to put her down when Gail's friends are around. As Jan leaves math class, Gail (in front of a bunch of her own friends) says to Jan: "Are you still crying to Mr. Jenks that the homework is too hard for your little brain?"

* Buck and Frank are competing for the starting spot on the varsity team. Frank approaches Buck in the locker room after practice and says, "I went out with your girl last night. She told me today how great it was to be with a *real* man."

* Lee is a different race (religion, ethnic background) from most of the students at school. A bunch of students descend on him after lunch and say, "Why don't you and your people just go back where you belong. Your kind isn't welcome here."

* Sarah's family is among the working poor. Her father is a dishwasher and her mother works part time at a local fast-food restaurant. Sarah is an excellent student, but is always overlooked. Today the guidance counselor just shook her head when Sarah inquired about college.

WORSHIP

Sing or say "I Want to Be Ready" (No. 151 in *Songs of Zion*).

Read aloud the call to worship. Have a leader read **Psalm 8:1** and the subsequent odd numbered verses. The other group members will read aloud the even verses.

Say the prayer of petition together. "O God, we thank you for naming us your children. Forgive us for those times when we have treated others as less than your image. Help us to remember that everyone is created in your image. May your Spirit strengthen us and make us determined to speak and to act toward one another in light of your image within all. Amen."

Sing "This Little Light of Mine" (No. 132 in *Songs of Zion*).

Share personal stories. This is an opportunity for group members to share their experience of what has happened in the group. Willing members should comment on their struggles with self-value, how they are dealing with the issue, or how they have dealt with it.

Close with a benediction.

Expelling the Monster From the Closet

by Natalie L. Woods

PURPOSE:

To help youth confront their personal fears and develop skills to cope with them, in both the social and the theological contexts.

PREPARATION

➡ List "Fear Situations" on newsprint. (See FYI.)

➡ Provide paper, pencil, and a Bible for each youth.

➡ Obtain from your local library a recorded (LP or cassette) version of the "Mountaintop" speech by Dr. Martin Luther King, Jr.

FOR YOUR INFORMATION

REAL FEARS

A point to be made is that there are both realistic fears and unrealistic fears. Realistic (or rational) fears usually produce a surge of adrenaline that helps us deal with a stressful situation. But at other times feeling afraid is simply the result of an unrealistic (or irrational) fear.

FEARS ARE REAL (15 minutes)

➡ Because fears are real, remind the group members to be sensitive to one another. Fears are not a laughing matter to the person involved. (See FYI.)

➡ Give each youth a sheet of paper and a pencil and point out the posted "Fear Situations."

➡ Ask each person to rank the whole list from "most fearful" to "least fearful." Take an inventory of the number of responses for each item to get a composite picture of the group's top five fears.

➡ Break into age-level groups and ask for volunteers to share a fear from their personal top five list and to tell about an irrational fear situation. Allow the other group members to question why the person was afraid and what can be done to alleviate this irrational fear.

RESPONSE TO FEAR
(25 minutes)

Older Youth

➠ Read **Proverbs 29:25** and **Psalm 27** (fear of others lays a snare) and **Romans 8:31-39** (if God is for us, who is against us?). Then discuss the following questions:

> Of the following, which is most like you and why: You are cautious in scary situations; you tend to stay afraid and let the situation get the better of you; or you don't let many things frighten you for long.
>
> What verse brings you the most assurance to face a fearful situation?
>
> How does faith in God help you conquer your fears?

Younger Youth

➠ Form small groups of one to four persons. Ask everyone to read **Romans 8:31-39**. Also assign one of the following passages to each group.

✝ **Exodus 3:1–4:17** (Moses responds to God.)
✝ **1 Samuel 17:1-50** (David faces Goliath.)
✝ **Matthew 14:22-23** (Peter walks on water.)
✝ **John 18:1-27** (Peter struggles.)

➠ Then discuss these questions:

> What was the fearful situation or the fear?
>
> How did each person deal with his or her fear?
>
> Did that person's faith play a significant part in conquering the fear? Why, or why not?
>
> What is worry? anxiety? fear? Are they all the same or different? How?
>
> What points are being made about conquering fear in **Romans 8:31-39**?
>
> Did your character utilize any of these points?
>
> Which of these verses would you commit to memory to use during your fearful times?

FEAR SITUATIONS

* low school performance/bad report card
* one's looks
* eating or drinking an unknown substance
* death of a parent
* sticking one's hand in a wriggling sack
* the possibility of violence at school
* losing a best friend
* walking across a deep body of water on a log or swinging bridge
* drugs and/or drinking
* bungee jumping
* making a public speech
* sexual abuse
* pregnancy or a sexually transmitted disease
* not fitting in
* being "found out"

RESPONDING TO FEAR

Dr. Martin Luther King, Jr., an African American minister, leader, and eloquent speaker for the civil rights movement that began in the United States during the 1950's, risked his life and career participating in nonviolent protests and preaching equality for all people.

Dr. King had been stabbed ten years before his death. The blade was so close to his aorta that if he'd sneezed, he would have died. Following that, he and his family faced many death and bombing threats.

It is ironic that Dr. King's "Mountaintop" speech was given the day before he was assassinated. Dr. King talked about the course of the civil rights movement from the student sit-ins, freedom rides, and the Birmingham bus boycott, to the Lincoln Memorial "I Have a Dream" demonstration and the Selma and Memphis movements.

Dr. King said, "Now, it doesn't matter. It really doesn't matter what happens now." He talked about a bomb threat on the plane that morning.

"I don't know what will happen now. We've got some difficult days ahead. But it really doesn't matter with me now. Because I've been to the mountaintop. Like anybody I would like to live a long life. Longevity has its place. But I'm not concerned about that now. I just want to do God's will. And He's allowed me to go up to the mountain. And I've looked over. And I've *seen* the Promised Land. And I may not get there with you. But I want you to know tonight that we as a people *will* get to the Promised Land. So I'm happy tonight. I'm not worried about *anything*. I'm not fearing *any* man.

"Mine eyes have seen the glory of the coming of the Lord. I have a

RESPONDING TO FEAR
(8 minutes)

➡ Let a volunteer read "Responding to Fear" to the group. (See FYI.) Then talk about these questions:

> What were some probable fears faced by Dr. King?
> Are these fears likely to be experienced by "ordinary people"? Why, or why not?
> What Scripture verses might have provided assurance to Martin Luther King, Jr.? What verses give you assurance?

FEAR INDEX (15 minutes)

When you are able to name your fear, you are then able to begin to overcome it. This next exercise is a continuation of the beginning exercise.

➡ Designate a place in the room that is the "I'm okay, this doesn't bother me" point. Have the group members line up shoulder-to-shoulder at this point.

➡ Review some of the techniques your group came up with for coping with fear during the "Fears Are Real" segment (page 24).

➡ Then read aloud the situations below. Ask at least five participants to step forward, indicating the degree of anxiety that one of the situations would produce. Ask volunteers to verbalize the fears involved with the situation. Feel free to expand this list.

➡ After reading aloud the following situations, discuss the group members' responses and what coping techniques might be useful. Help the participants to see that fear is a common emotion and that the same situation can affect each person differently.

* You have been asked to give a seven-minute speech during your school's assembly next week.

* The morning news informs your city that Cure-All headache medication, batch #4508, has been found to contain a deadly substance. You took two tablets from that batch last night.

* Your parents are out of town and your house's security alarm sounds off at 3:00 A.M.

* Your teacher informs you that out of a class of thirty students, only five passed the course.

* You finally have your parent's car by yourself and you realize that you are thirty miles over the speed limit the same instant you see the "you may resume your speed" school zone sign and the police car.

dream this afternoon that the brotherhood of man will become a reality. With this faith, *I* will go out and carve a tunnel of hope from a mountain of despair . . . . With this faith, *we* will be able to achieve this new day, when all of God's children—black men and white men, Jews and Gentiles, Protestants and Catholics—will be able to join hands and sing with the Negroes in the spiritual of old, 'Free at last! Free at last! Thank God almighty we are free at last!'"
(From *Let the Trumpet Sound: The Life of Martin Luther King, Jr.*, by Stephen B. Oates; Harper & Row, 1982; pages 485–86.)

WORSHIP

Assign volunteers verses from **Psalm 27**. Give them time to read through their verses silently. Let the group know that the reading of **Psalm 27** will be the closing prayer for this session.

Begin with silent prayer. Request that everyone give thanks and praise to God for all of God's goodness.

Listen to the "Mountaintop" speech. Play the ending of the recorded version of Dr. King's "Mountaintop" speech, including the portion mentioned above.

Read the psalm. Have the volunteers read aloud **Psalm 27** with the feeling David might have had when he wrote these verses. At the conclusion have everyone say "Amen."

Resources for Youth

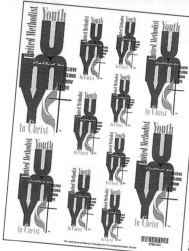

UMY OFFICIAL LOGO CLIP ART.
Everybody needs to know! And now you can tell them easily. Use the United Methodist official logo clip art sheets to dress up your newsletters, announcements, bulletins, and more! 5 sheets per package; varied sizes. #78218X. **$1.50**

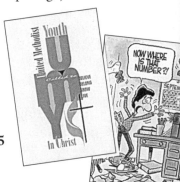

UMY CARDS.
Jot a quick note to let them know what's on your mind. These cards serve as reminders, pep talks, news notices, and requests for prayer.
Per 100, **$8.50;** Per 25, **$2.25**
#322227. **Meeting/Event Notice Card**
#322235. **UMY Logo Card**
#322243. **Camping Logo Card**
#322251. *NEW!* **YSF Logo Card**

Y! WEAR.
Youth can speak up for faith!

Y! Wear echoes the UMC's vision for youth ministry: Called to believe, belong, grow, live in Christ! This witness wear collection is available in three colors:

UMY T-Shirt: White
#322215. Medium. **$11.95**
#322226. Large. **$11.95**
#322237. XL. **$11.95**
#323128. XXL. **$12.95**

UMY T-Shirt: Gray
#322272. Medium. **$11.95**
#322283. Large. **$11.95**
#322306. XL. **$11.95**
#323130. XXL. **$12.95**

UMY T-Shirt: Black
#322248. Medium. **$11.95**
#322250. Large. **$11.95**   #322261. XL. **$11.95**
#323117. XXL. **$12.95**

Call for Information About New Y-Wear Designs.

UMY STICKERS. Stick up for what's important! UMY Stickers are great for group identity conversations with someone outside the church and for consciousness-raising that leads to fundraising! Stickers come in rolls of 100 and are available individually from Cokesbury stores.
#319456. Per 100, **$6.35;** Per 500, **$29.25;** Per 1000, **$52.50**

THE UNITED METHODIST YOUTH FELLOWSHIP HANDBOOK.
✻ **For Junior and Senior Highs and adults who work with youth**
✻ **UM-approved resource**
✻ **Basic Resource: 220-page handbook**

Here's the basic resource for creating or recreating the youth fellowship group. There is information on every aspect of forming and maintaining an effective youth group. Directions for comprehensive leadership includes the areas of community service, worship, music, Bible study, work camp, fellowship, and fundraising. This Handbook contains a chapter devoted solely to the Junior High UMYF in ministry, and another to the Senior High UMYF. The Handbook also covers the combined group. This Handbook is a must for anyone who has contact with the youth group—pastors, group officers, and adult leaders.
#057621. **$15.95**

Cokesbury

CALL OR VISIT YOUR COKESBURY STORE

ORDER TOLL FREE: 1-800-672-1789

28

Satisfaction Guaranteed!
Prices subject to change without notice. Shipping and handling extra.

CHURCH ISSUES

What I Would Love to Hear in Church

by Natalie L. Woods

▶ PURPOSE:

To help youth think about, evaluate, articulate, and ask for from the worship committee or the pastor what they want and need to know and understand in church about all facets of worship, particularly concerning their spiritual needs and current youth issues.

▶ PREPARATION

➠ Bring a collection of bulletins from your church's worship services and a copy of *The United Methodist Hymnal* for each participant.

➠ If possible, gather other worship resources that your group uses, such as *Songs of Zion*, *Youth! Praise* cassettes or CD's, or other liturgical sources.

FOR YOUR INFORMATION

ORDER OF WORSHIP

Many United Methodist churches use the recommended order of worship as presented in "The Basic Pattern of Worship" on pages 2–5 of *The United Methodist Hymnal*. Notice that there are four basic components to worship: Entrance, Proclamation and Response, Thanksgiving and Communion, and Sending Forth.

WORSHIP: RITUALS WITH PURPOSE (20 minutes)

➠ Form groups of three or four persons. Give each group a bulletin, a pencil, and a hymnal.

➠ Have each group identify the four basic components of their church's worship service. They should note what rituals are performed as a part of each component and then talk about what part each ritual plays in the role of worship. (See FYI.)

➠ Identify also the parts of worship in which youth along with the entire congregation are active participants. Then discuss the following questions:

How much of the worship service do **you** actively participate in?

Is there any part of the worship that you do not understand? If so, what? Why, do you think?

Is there a part of worship that adds to your feeling of worship during the service? What part?

Is there a part of the worship that detracts from your feeling of worship during the service? What part?

WORSHIP IN THE BIBLE
(20 minutes)

➡ Form age-level groups and ask for a volunteer reader in each group.

➡ Group members will mill around the room while listening to the Scripture. When the reader pauses, participants will form a lifelike group pose demonstrating how they think they or someone else would be feeling or behaving in that particular situation. (See FYI.)

Older Youth

➡ Assign **Psalm 100**. The participants may consider this psalm as a call to worship or even as a liturgical dance interpretation that would be appropriate for Sunday morning worship.

➡ Debrief the experience by discussing the psalm's attitude, the actions of worship in the psalm, and how this psalm is alike or different from the group members' personal experiences.

Younger Youth

➡ Assign **Acts 2:40-47**, which talks about the fellowship that members of the early church experienced in their daily lives. The Scripture may need to be read twice for understanding by the group. ("He" in verse 40 is Peter.)

➡ You may decide to debrief as you go along or at the end of the Scripture passage to make sure everyone is following the interpretations. Then ask:

> What part did worship play in this community of Christians?
> What kinds of things were believers doing as part of their worship?
> What same kinds of actions are believers doing in the modern church?

BIBLICAL WORSHIP

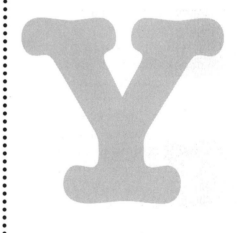

People throughout history have found ways to celebrate God in their midst through worship. As Christians we stand in the tradition celebrated in Hebrew festivals of the Old Testament and in celebrations of the early church.

Worship is a primary gathering of the community of Christians in which persons of all ages are given an opportunity to pray, worship, sing, and be challenged to love and serve God and neighbor.

THE PRACTICE OF WORSHIP

Making worship "come alive" is the key for spiritual revival in youth. Some elements of worship include kneeling, chanting, ritual, lavish display and dedication of wealth, altar prayer, personal prayer, song, dance, reading of Scripture, preaching from Scripture, celebration of baptism, and the celebration of Communion. These elements may be used singly or combined.

It is the responsibility of the pastor, often in conjunction with the music director and the worship committee, to design worship services that enable people to participate in worship and to grow in faith.

Given the opportunity to participate in worship, youth will feel they are an important part of the life of their church, and can play a part in helping to make worship relevant. The youth will feel connected with faithful worshipers in their congregation and throughout history.

PRACTICE AND STRATEGY IN WORSHIP (20-30 minutes)

➠ Review the FYI information on the practice of worship and ask:

> What would you like to see added to your church's worship that would make it more meaningful to you?
> How can youth ask to become a part of the planning and/or "doing" of worship?
> Do you know who is responsible for or whom to go to with requests for changes in the Order of Worship in your church (*start with the pastor or the worship committee chairperson*)?
> What worship resources are meaningful to you that you could introduce to the rest of the congregation?

➠ In a group brainstorming session, identify what changes, additions, or deletions participants would like to see in the worship to make it more "youth friendly."

➠ Strategize the best ways to approach the pastor and worship committee of your church to initiate changes to make your worship more "youth friendly." Some suggestions follow.

* Identify portions of *The United Methodist Hymnal* and *The Book of Worship* as well as other resources like *Youth! Praise* that you would like to suggest for future worship services.

* Set a time and place for the youth to meet with the pastor and others involved in designing worship and explore together an ongoing way to be involved in the worship experience of your church. This can include anything that goes on during worship or that supports the worship (such as ushers, greeters, baking Communion bread, preparation of the sanctuary, and so on).

* Present your requests for worship at this time. Be prepared to demonstrate liturgical dance, *Youth! Praise* music, or any other requests that may be new or different from the regular worship service.

* Explore other ideas for worship that might be effective. (See "Ideas for Future Worship," page 33.)

IDEAS FOR FUTURE WORSHIP

The United Methodist Hymnal and *The Book of Worship* have a variety of multicultural expressions of worship: songs, affirmations of faith, hymns, prayers, and more.

* Read aloud **Psalm 150** with pauses for group poses. How can this "action" psalm be presented by the youth as a call to worship on Sunday morning? Is this an option that your group would like to pursue? If so, plan your action.

* Read aloud **Colossians 3:12-17**, which gives guidance for the life of the community. Allow pauses for group interpretation in poses. Then ask: Are there other ways in which you would like to have an opportunity to pray, worship, or sing in your congregational worship experience? If so, what? How creative are you in challenging other teens to love and serve God and neighbor through worship?

* *Optional:* Recreate a worship service of the early church through costumes and traditional customs for presentation at a congregational worship service.

WORSHIP

Begin with a choral reading. Use "This Is the Day" (No. 657 in *The United Methodist Hymnal*). Instead of singing it, speak the words as a chorus.

Present a psalm. Present **Psalm 23** in an innovative way: signing, liturgical dance, free interpretation.

Pray together. Ask the participants to mention their joys and concerns. Have everyone respond with "Hear our prayer, O Lord."

Invite the telling of a personal story. Ask a volunteer to share his or her witness to God.

Sing or say "This Is the Day" (No. 657 in the *Hymnal*).

Worship: Offering My Giftedness to God

by David F. White

PURPOSE:

To help youth reflect on their own participation in worship and in the leadership and design of worship, both with and for the congregation and in their own space.

PREPARATION

➡ Invite a worship leader or some other member of the church to explain the order of worship for your congregation.

➡ Become familiar with the stories "Thanking God for Deliverance" (page 36) and "Phillip's Egg" (page 37).

➡ For the "Gift Hunt" prepare a list of ten common items that teenagers might have with them in a youth meeting.

➡ Have two or three youth observe a previous Sunday morning worship service, noticing feelings as well as sights, sounds, and senses.

➡ Assemble Bibles, poster paper, magazines, newspapers, glue, markers, and other materials for the collage. For worship gather a candle, matches, and copies of *The United Methodist Hymnal*.

FOR YOUR INFORMATION

GIFT HUNT: PART TWO

If the teams without adults are too uneven, switch a few people to equalize the teams.

Each team will cooperate to write a brief story (about anything), but they must mention each one of the items used independently by their team during the first part. They need not have scored a point for the item.

Ask each team to read its completed story for the whole group.

GIFT HUNT (10 minutes)

➡ Form equal groups of three to seven persons, including adults. The groups should be scattered about the room an equal distance from the center, where the leader will stand. Stage this game as a competition.

➡ Instruct each team to choose a runner who will bring the items called for to the center of the room. After each item is called out, the first team to place it in the leader's hand will get a point.

➡ The team with the most points will win the first half of the game. The items from each team should be set aside and saved for the second half of the game.

➡ For the second half of the game, teens only will work together to create a story using the items that they offered in the first half of the game. (See FYI.)

➡ After the game, ask the questions on page 35.

Did all the participants freely offer items that they had in their possession?

Was there any team that scored solely on the contributions of one person? If so, how did the other team members feel?

In writing the stories, what gifts did you see emerging in each participant?

Does this game remind you of worship with the congregation? Why, or why not?

INTERVIEWS (10 minutes)

➠ Conduct an interview with the three youth who observed worship. Ask the following questions "Oprah" style:

What sights, sounds, smells, or sensations made more of an impression on you? Why, do you think?

Have you been to worship services in other churches?

How are other services both alike and different from our own?

Did you have a sense of God's presence? If so, in what parts of the service? If not, why, do you think?

How did you feel in each part of the service?

In what parts of the service were youth most active? (Remember that persons in the pews are also participants in some way.)

If youth were not involved, why not, do you think?

What do you as a teenager think youth have to offer in worship?

WHAT DOES IT ALL MEAN?
(20 minutes)

➠ Invite the pastor or lay leader to hand out sample worship bulletins and explain some of the elements of your congregation's worship services. (See FYI for a listing of some of the worship elements.) Allow some time for questions and discussion.

SOME WORSHIP (OR LITURGICAL) ELEMENTS

Prelude/Postlude
Call to Worship

Hymns
* praise
* dedication
* commitment

Passing of the peace
Scripture readings

Special music or other arts
* handbell choir
* instrumental music
* vocal choirs
* solos
* liturgical dance

Prayer concerns of the people
* pastoral prayer
* Lord's Prayer

Sermon (proclamation)
* children's sermon

Offering of tithes and gifts
* call to discipleship

Sacraments
* Holy Communion
* baptism

Benediction

THANKING GOD FOR DELIVERANCE

Long ago when the Hebrew people were enslaved by the Egyptians and forced to work long hours without food or rest, God sent Moses to ask Pharaoh to let the people go. God heard their cry and had compassion on these slaves. God intended to release them from bondage (Exodus 3:7-12). The purpose given to Pharaoh for their release was to go into the wilderness and hold a worship festival to God (Exodus 5:1).

When Pharaoh repeatedly refused, God sent many plagues on the Egyptians, finally forcing them to let the Hebrew children go with Moses to a new land.

As they wandered in the wilderness outside Egypt, God gave them food, water, and protection on their way to the new land of Canaan. When they had come to the mountain called Sinai, God gave them a number of laws and commandments to help them live a life of closeness and obedience to God.

It was to thank God for God's deliverance, protection, and love that the people of Israel built a tabernacle and worshiped God. Exodus 35:20-29 is the story of how the people all gathered their own possessions and gave them to build a place of worship for God.

HOW DOES THE BIBLE ADDRESS WORSHIP? (10 minutes)

Older Youth

➡ Read aloud or tell in your own words the story "Thanking God for Deliverance" or ask a volunteer. (See FYI.)

➡ Then read aloud Exodus 35:20-29.

➡ Discuss the following questions:

> What is the purpose of worship?
> What gifts did the Israelites bring?
> Why did the people bring gifts? What was their attitude? How do you think each person decided what to bring?
> What do you think this has to say about what we bring to worship?
> Do you think God wants us to bring more than our things to worship? If so, what else could we bring?

Younger Youth

➡ Have the participants form teams and read aloud Psalm 95:1-7.

➡ Ask the group members to create a collage using pictures from magazines and newspapers that illustrate some of the ways in which they envision worship in this psalm.

➡ Ask the participants to talk about their collages and then to answer these questions:

> What do you think is the purpose of worship?
> What can we bring to worship besides our money for the offering?
> What could you bring to a worship service that would help it make sense and be meaningful to you?

BEGIN TO PLAN A WORSHIP SERVICE (15 minutes)

➡ Brainstorm a list of talents each person has, remembering that "behind the scenes" talents are equally as valuable as the "up front" talents. Record the list on poster paper.

➡ Ask the group members to assess their gifts in light of the "worship element" list and the explanations of the guest speaker. Talk about who can read well out loud, who plans well, who writes well, who sings, who can usher, and so on. (See "Phillip's Egg" on page 37.)

→ After assessing the parts of worship and the contributions each person can make, divide into two work groups.

→ Team one will work on the liturgy—the order of worship, selecting songs and hymns, prayers, and so on.

→ Team two will work on the form and content of the proclamation (the sermon in some form). This segment includes the Scripture, since the proclamation is based on it.

→ The service needs a balance between hearing from God (Scripture, sermon, some music, and so on) and responding to God (some music, prayers, affirmations, offertory, call to discipleship, and so on).

PHILLIP'S EGG

Phillip was a ten-year-old boy with Down syndrome. He also was a member of a Sunday school class where he was treated unkindly and mocked for his different speech and his inability to participate in all the class's activities. One Easter the teacher handed out large plastic eggs and asked each student to fill his or her egg with a symbol of life. The students scattered all about the outside of the church and began searching. When they had all gathered again, the teacher asked them to open their eggs and share with the class what they had found.

The first student to share offered a beautiful butterfly because it had grown from a caterpillar. The second student offered a leaf because it had recently came from a tree that was bare.

When Phillip's turn came, he opened the egg and it was empty. All the other students laughed and some ridiculed him saying, "You never do anything like you are supposed to!" But Phillip answered, "I did too! The egg is empty because Jesus' tomb was empty and he is alive again!" As Phillip finished his explanation the class found their differences melt away into acceptance.

A few months later the class was saddened to hear of Phillip's death. At the funeral each student placed an empty egg on his casket as a symbol because Phillip was no longer sealed in the tomb of his difference. In the new life that Christ offered Phillip, the children found they could accept one another even as God accepted each of their gifts. (Adapted from a story in *Pockets* magazine, © The Upper Room, April 1987, from a sermon by Rev. Harry H. Pritchett, Jr., All Saints Church, Atlanta, Georgia.)

WORSHIP

Sing "Here I Am, Lord" (No. 593 in *The United Methodist Hymnal*).

Find a symbol of worship. Ask all the group members to either go outside or around the room to find one symbol of how God speaks to them or how they hear God's voice.

Gather in a circle. As the group gathers, lower the lights and use a single candle in the middle.

Offer a witness of God's presence. Only the person who holds the candle may speak out of respect for the voice of God in that person.

Pass the candle around the circle; the person holding the candle may speak or pass. Each speaker may share with the group how he or she hears God speaking through his or her symbol.

The worship leader may change the topic (for example "How have you heard God speaking in other people?" or "What do you feel called to give back to God?").

Close with the song "Alleluia" (No. 186 in the *Hymnal*).

The Twelve Were Only the Beginning

by Linda L. Pickens-Jones

PURPOSE:

To help youth learn some biblical concepts of discipleship, understand themselves as significant and active members of the church, develop a plan of discipleship for their own church life, and identify ways to continue in a life of discipleship.

PREPARATION

➡ Have a Bible and a copy of *The United Methodist Hymnal* for each person, a copy of the *Book of Discipline*, and commentaries on Matthew, Mark, Luke, and John.
➡ Gather paper, pencils, and two leaf-shaped pieces of paper for each person.
➡ Prepare the drawing of the vine. (See FYI.)
➡ Have on hand large sheets of butcher paper or newsprint and crayons or markers (a different color for each person, if possible).

FOR YOUR INFORMATION

THE VINE

Prepare the picture of the vine and branches. On a large sheet of paper, such as newsprint, draw a vine with lots of branches. This doesn't need to be a perfect piece of art! Post it on the wall of the meeting room.

Cut realistic-sized leaf shapes from green paper, with a design simple enough to use a paper cutter (or one that volunteers can prepare ahead of time). Make two or three for each group member. These will be used once in the program and again during worship.

THE BEGINNING: WHO ARE THE DISCIPLES? (10 minutes)

➡ Form groups of two to four persons and assign each group at least one of the following Bible passages. Distribute Bibles, paper, and pencils.

✝ **Matthew 8:14-17** (Jesus visits Peter's house.)
✝ **Matthew 10:5-15** (Jesus sends the disciples.)
✝ **Matthew 18:21-22** (Jesus speaks on forgiveness.)
✝ **Mark 8:34-35** (instructions to followers)
✝ **Mark 12:41-44** (Jesus in the Temple)
✝ **Luke 5:17-20** (Jesus and the paralyzed man)
✝ **Luke 10:29-37** (Jesus tells a parable.)
✝ **Luke 13:10-13** (Jesus and the crippled woman)
✝ **John 6:1-14** (Jesus at the Sea of Galilee)

➡ Ask each group to read their assigned Scripture. On one side of the paper, the participants are to identify and write down the names of the disciples. On the other side of the paper, everyone is to write down what the disciples are doing in the story. Ask the groups to compare notes with one another.

➡ Give each person a leaf-shaped piece of paper. Ask the participants to write on the paper one word or short phrase that describes an action of one of the disciples that they liked or were particularly interested in from the story, such as feeding, healing, teaching, and so on.

➡ Have the group members reflect on what they have learned about the actions of disciples, and then place their leaves on the posted picture of the vine and branches. (See FYI information on how to make the vine.)

JESUS' IDEA OF DISCIPLESHIP (10-15 minutes)

➡ Have a volunteer summarize the picture of discipleship painted by Jesus in **John 15:1-17**. (See FYI.)

➡ Brainstorm some ideas that use contemporary images for the ideas Jesus is expressing.

➡ Divide into groups of six to eight persons. Each group will create a "movement machine," which shows the idea of being connected, of each person having a part, and of each making a difference.

➡ Each group will demonstrate its machine to the entire group. Then talk about the following questions:

> How did the machines that were created and the image of vine and branches help you see the importance of being connected?
> Why do you think we disciples need to be connected? What connects us?
> Do you think you have any way to make a difference? Why, or why not?
> Do you think "just being" a disciple counts for anything? Give a reason for your answer.

JESUS' IDEA OF DISCIPLESHIP

We see from this program that there are many kinds of disciples and that their actions reach out in many directions. One of the ways to talk about being disciples is described in **John 15**. Jesus called God the "vinegrower," himself the "true vine," and those who live in the ways of Christ "the branches."

These branches are to bear fruit: to produce something, not just to sit there. The ability to do something and to care happens through the love of God and of one another. The word Jesus uses to summarize all of this is that we are called to be "friends." When we are baptized and when we join the local church through confirmation, we indicate that we have accepted God's love and that we have agreed to act out the love of God. Jesus describes us as friends who branch out in acts of discipleship, born of love.

PROMISES OF JESUS' FRIENDS

We promise at the time we join a local church to support it in several ways. We are asked, "Do you promise, according to the grace given you, to keep God's holy will and commandments and walk in the same all the days of your life as *faithful members* of Christ's holy church?" (From *The United Methodist Hymnal*, 1989; page 47.)

As United Methodists we commit ourselves to serving Christ and the church through the support of our "prayers, presence, gifts, and service." The vows of confirmation are found in the Baptismal Covenant III in *The United Methodist Hymnal*.

YOUTH ARE CHURCH MEMBERS TOO

"Youth who are full members of the church have all rights and responsibilities of church membership." (From *The Book of Discipline of The United Methodist Church*, 1992; page 126.)

Look for some ways to help the group identify the rights and responsibilities of church membership as they observe them in the life of the local church.

WE HAVE PROMISED TO BE JESUS' FRIENDS! (8-10 minutes)

➠ Place very large sheets of butcher paper or newsprint on the floor. Each paper should have one of the following words written on it: *Prayers, Presence, Gifts,* or *Service.* Clarify what these words mean. (See FYI.)

➠ Provide a different color marker or crayon for each person. Work in teams of two or three persons, if you prefer.

➠ Give each person or team four minutes to think of and write down all the ways that the youth group, the church, or individuals in the church fulfill their membership vows of supporting The United Methodist Church with their prayers, presence, gifts, or service.

➠ When time is called, summarize the group's findings. Then discuss these questions:

> What gifts of your own did you identify? What kinds of service?
>
> How do you think prayer can help the church? Do you believe that prayer "works"? Give reasons for your answers.
>
> Do you think the "size" of the gift, time commitment, or service offered makes a difference to God? to your local church? (For example, does God appreciate $100 more than $2 or one year of Sunday school teaching more than ten hours of child care in the nursery?) Give reasons for your answer.

YOUTH *ARE* CHURCH MEMBERS (10-15 minutes)

➠ Investigate how the group members can work within the church to be better disciples who have "membership privileges" just as the adults do. (See FYI.)

➠ Divide into age-level groups to do the idea generation and nomination of planning team representatives.

➠ Before the age-level groups do their work, ask these questions:

> Can you see yourself as an active and significant member of this church? Do you see yourself as a disciple? Why, or why not?
>
> What, do you think, are the rights and responsibilities of discipleship? of church membership?
>
> How are those rights and responsibilities the same? different?

Older Youth

⟹ Form four groups and assign one category to each group: prayers, presence, gifts, or service.

⟹ Each group should discuss a way that the youth group can be more involved in this area. The ideas can include ways the teens can do something on their own or ways they can get the whole church to be involved.

⟹ Share the decisions with the whole group. Discuss and help the group reach a consensus as to what they will be committed to.

⟹ Choose a plan and/or a time for the whole group to follow through on their commitments. (Try to do this soon!)

Younger Youth

⟹ For each category (prayers, presence, gifts, service) ask each person to come up with some ideas about how individuals or group members could be more involved as disciples in their own local church.

⟹ Ask each person to choose his or her favorite action for each category. Tally the choices and ask the group to think of one or two to address first.

⟹ If you have time, begin to think of specific plans for how to be involved in that area. Nominate a few members to work on a planning group to follow through on developing plans for each of the four areas of commitment.

WORSHIP

The worship segment will provide an opportunity for each individual to respond to the call to discipleship.

Sing or say "Spirit of the Living God" (No. 393 in *The United Methodist Hymnal*).

Read John 15:1-5 and 12-15. Ask two volunteers to read aloud the separate passages.

Present your intentions for discipleship. Give each person another "leaf." Remind the group members of their promises of prayers, presence, gifts, and service. Ask each person to write one thing he or she intends to do as one of Jesus' friends. When ready, each person should take the leaf and place it on the "vine and branches" poster.

Offer thanks. Read in unison "Thanksgiving" from the Baptismal Covenant IV (page 52 in the *Hymnal*).

Sing or say a hymn of commitment from the *Hymnal*, such as "Here I Am, Lord" (No. 593) or "Sois la Semilla" (No. 583).

Commiting to Christ

by David F. White

PURPOSE:

To help youth think carefully and theologically about their relationship to Jesus Christ and make a meaningful commitment to Christ (in their own time and at their own level of spiritual and emotional development).

PREPARATION

➠ Gather ten or twelve cardboard tissue tubes or building blocks and two pieces of construction paper for each person, tape or glue, paper and pencils, Bibles, copies of *The United Methodist Hymnal*, and commentaries for Exodus, Matthew, Mark, and Luke. Be sure to also bring a CD/cassette player and a copy of *Youth! Praise* for the worship segment.

➠ Have available poster paper and markers or a chalkboard and chalk.

➠ Invite five or six adults or youth who can tell how they worked through doubts in their faith and how they maintain their commitment to Jesus Christ.

FOR YOUR INFORMATION

BUILDING A FAITH HOUSE

Use the statements from the Apostles' Creed, as well as the words from the "Renunciation" in the Baptismal Covenant I, page 34 in *The United Methodist Hymnal*. Write the statements in coherent sentences on paper squares and tape them to the tubes or the building blocks.

Group members will use the tubes to build a foundation of faith categories. Place the construction paper on top of erect tubes and build as many tiers as you wish.

Builders should represent in some manner the most and least

YOUR HOUSE OF FAITH
(15 minutes)

Older Youth

➠ Appoint a scribe and ask the participants to recite as much as they know of the Apostles' Creed. The scribe will write it on the poster paper. If you need to, check it in *The United Methodist Hymnal*, No. 881 or 882.

➠ Have the group members build a representation of what they believe (or think they believe or want to believe), using elements of the Creed or other faith statements. (See FYI, "Building a Faith House.")

➠ Then ask these questions:

What are the most important elements?
What are the least important?
How would the Christian faith change without some of the elements? God the Father? Jesus Christ? the holy catholic church? forgiveness?

→ After the discussion ask group members to demonstrate areas in which they have questions or doubts by removing the tubes or blocks that refer to those faith statements.

→ Some structures may wobble or fall. Ask the participants to walk about and find others who have similar "tubes of doubt" as themselves. This will form groups in which they will move about the room in the next exercise.

Younger Youth

→ Set up two opposite sides of the rooms representing a range of strong belief to unbelief. Post signs to indicate the poles. The area between is for the range of belief between the extremes.

→ Use the "Pole Position Statements" to illustrate what group members strongly believe or have the greatest doubts about. (See FYI, page 44.)

→ After moving to register belief or doubt, talk about why group members believe as they do.

important elements to them. For example, the bottom may represent the most important elements: Belief in God, in Jesus, and in the Spirit. The top tier of columns may represent beliefs that they see as less important. The top of each structure may resemble a pitched roof with the builder's name(s) written on it.

Note these samples of statements for the tubes:

The Apostles' Creed
1. I believe in God the Father Almighty.
2. I believe God is creator of heaven and earth.
3. I believe Jesus Christ is God's only Son our Lord.
4. I believe in the Holy Spirit.
5. I believe in the holy catholic [universal] church.
6. I believe in the forgiveness of sins.

Baptismal Covenant I
1. I renounce the spiritual forces of wickedness.
2. I reject the evil powers of this world.
3. I repent of my sin.
4. I promise to serve Jesus Christ as Lord, in union with the Church which Christ has opened to people of all ages, nations, and races.

POLE POSITION STATEMENTS

1. I believe that the Bible is the testimony about God's will for us.
2. I believe that God is a person who loves and cares for us.
3. I believe that Jesus Christ is God's Son and our Savior.
4. I believe that the Holy Spirit is a helper to us giving us God's comfort and wisdom.
5. I believe that it is God's will that I commit to the church as God's people.
6. I believe that being Christian means doing God's will in keeping commandments.
7. I believe that being Christian means helping others in doing justice and helping the poor.
8. I believe in heaven as an eternity of love and peace with God.

QUESTIONING STATIONS
(20 minutes)

➡ Station around the room adults or youth who can discuss specific topics about which they have had doubt, concerning topics such as God, Jesus, the church, salvation, future judgment, and so on. It is important that these persons also feel free to say that they don't know all the answers and that they still struggle with faith questions.

➡ Ask these persons to share ways in which they have worked through some of their faith struggles. Allow some time for the group members to discuss their doubts. (Warning: This should not become a confrontational or combative experience, nor a time for persons to give the "answers" to teens, but rather a warm sharing of questions.)

FAITHFULNESS IN THE BIBLE
(15 minutes)

➡ Distribute Bibles and commentaries. The passages that follow speak about some of the requirements for commitment to God, as well as some of the struggles to maintain those commitments.

➡ Ask the group members to look up their Scripture passages in the Bible and a commentary; or, assign a different passage to each of three smaller groups.

➡ After they have studied the passages, ask the participants to complete these sentence stems:

* Sometimes keeping my faith requires . . .
* Sometimes it is a struggle to keep my faith commitment because . . .
* Even Jesus had difficulty when . . .
* Something that helps strengthen my faith commitment is . . .
* When I realize prominent people in the Bible had doubts and fears about their faith, I feel . . .

Older Youth
✝ **Exodus 6:28-7:7** (Moses and Aaron are called by God.)
✝ **Matthew 27:45-50** (Jesus on the cross)
✝ **Luke 18:18-25** (the rich ruler)

Younger Youth
✝ **Matthew 4:1-11** (the temptation of Jesus)
✝ **Matthew 7:24-29** (house built on rock or sand)
✝ **Matthew 26:36-46** (Jesus in Gethsemane)

REWRITING THE AFFIRMATION
(5 minutes)

➡ In closing ask the participants to write their own affirmation of faith. They should include those things that they believe about their faith. Each affirmation should begin with "I believe in . . . " You may want to post these expressions of faith on the walls of your youth room.

WORSHIP

Gather with the "house of faith" building blocks. Ask the participants to bring the tubes of unbelief from their houses of faith. Place these tubes in the center of the circle.

Talk more about specific questions. Ask the youth to tell what they still have questions or doubts about. Ask them also to talk about ways in which sharing with others who have doubts may have helped them.

Read aloud Mark 9:24 and talk about what the passage means.

Encourage a commitment. Challenge the youth to commit their doubts and questions to God, to believe, and to ask God to help them—starting where they are now—with their unbelief.

Spend time in silent meditation. Ask the group members to consider silently what they do know of their faith. Ask them to picture what their life would be like if they lived according to what they felt confident of.

Close by singing "Here I Am, Lord" from *Youth! Praise.*

Just say *ahhhhh*...

Is your youth group ready for its annual checkup?

You know that if it goes unchecked, your youth group could become unhealthy. That's why *The Complete Youth Group Checkup* helps you doctor your group by examining its reflexes and pressure points. Think about it—how is *your* youth group doing on
◆ building a community of trust?
◆ growing spiritually?
◆ avoiding catching an *ism*?
◆ responding to persons who need love and care?
◆ making decisions about their lives?

With positive approaches and a healthy dose of faith, *The Complete Youth Group Checkup* is chock-full of fantastic ideas plus:
◆ adaptable schedules and planning guides for effective retreats
◆ helps for older youth and younger youth
◆ worship that's integrated with the topic
◆ creative and meaningful activities
◆ and more!

Get a "shot in the arm" with these great youth programs!

Is My Nose Growing and 29 Other Great Youth Programs helps you tackle difficult issues with an upbeat approach. And don't worry about *Is My Nose Growing* being stuffy—everyone will relate to the contemporary images and examples. Best of all, each program shows how to make the Bible relevant to decisions youth face every day. Topics include:
◆ Do the Good Guys Ever Win?
◆ I Don't Like it When You Do That
◆ Can God Forgive Me?
◆ Am I Manipulated by Advertising?
◆ Showing Your Family You Love Them
◆ Who Is My Enemy?
◆ Resisting Injustice
◆ Praying for Others
◆ What's the Fuss About Lyrics?
◆ Bumper Sticker Values

Help your youth group become healthier and call or visit Cokesbury today!
The Complete Youth Group Checkup. CA4-361710
Is My Nose Growing? CA4-197074

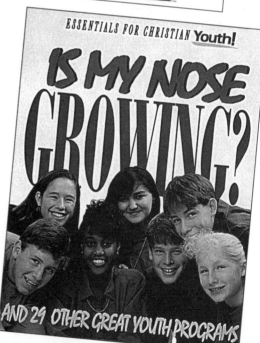

CALL OR VISIT YOUR COKESBURY STORE

ORDER TOLL FREE: 1-800-672-1789

• • •

Satisfaction Guaranteed!
Prices subject to change without notice. Shipping and handling extra.

UPA-139-4

SOCIAL ISSUES

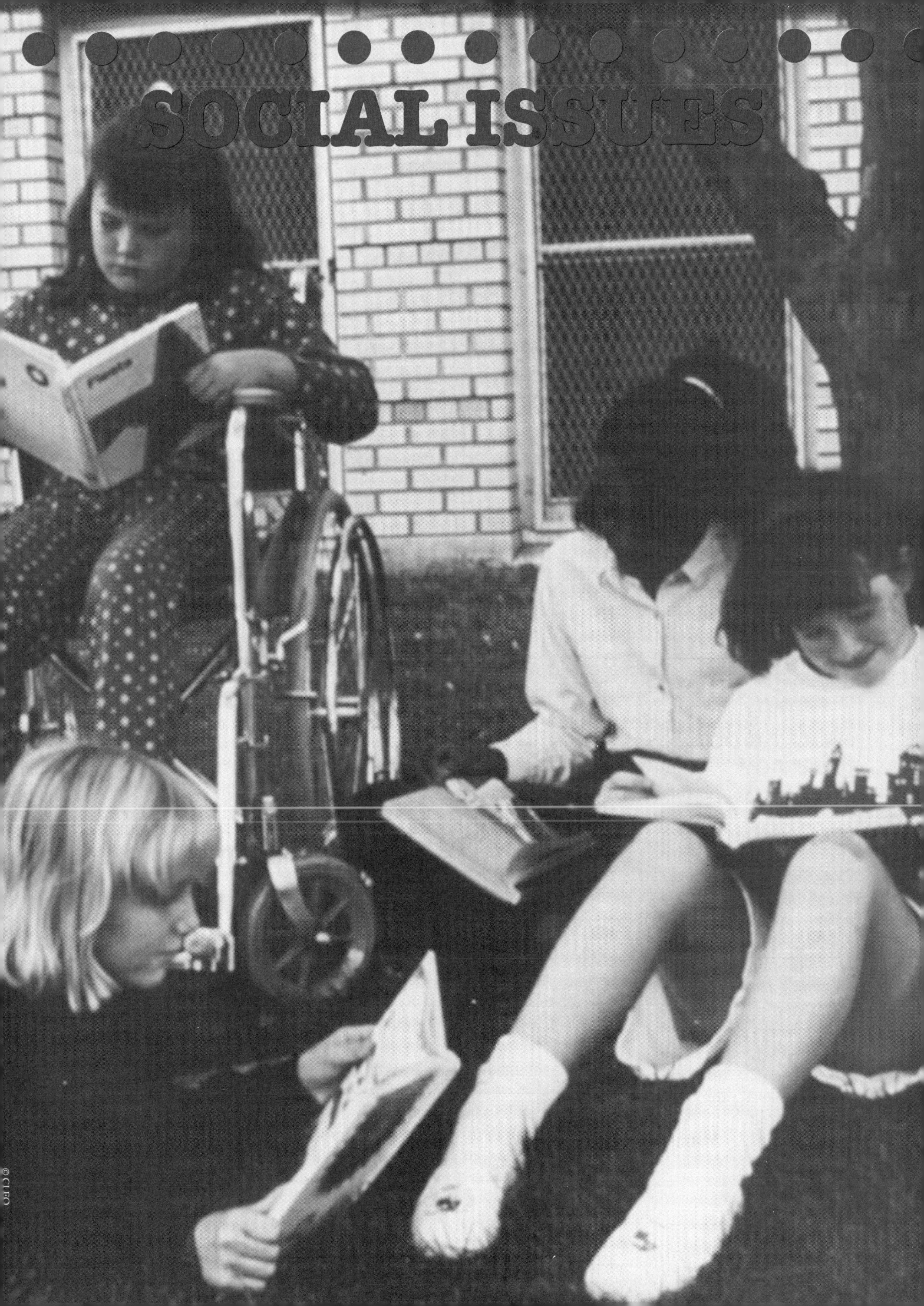

©CLEO

Did You Hear What Happened to . . . ?

by David F. White

▶ **PURPOSE:**

The purpose of this program is to help youth understand the insidious effects of gossip, why it is so attractive, and what the Bible says about gossip and "false witness."

▶ **PREPARATION**

➥ Prepare labels with negative character traits.
➥ Photocopy the gossip situations and cut and paste them onto index cards.
➥ Gather newsprint, markers, paper, pencils, *Supplement to the Book of Hymns*, and Bibles.

FOR YOUR INFORMATION

WHAT WOULD YOU DO?

The following examples should make youth consider what is and is not gossip and why.

---

* Ty has a great new pair of pump athletic shoes, which would be difficult at best for him to afford, even though he has a job. This morning Denny, one of Ty's rivals for a starting spot on the basketball team, heard a couple of people wondering out loud where Ty got the shoes. This afternoon Denny heard several other people saying that Ty stole them. At practice Denny told Ty what he heard.

CREATING REPUTATIONS (10 minutes)

➥ As the group members enter the room, tape a label on each one's back. The label will be known and visible only to others. (No peeking; no telling!) Instruct the participants to treat each person as if he or she really has the character trait that the label implies.

➥ With the labels in place, ask for volunteers to guess what they believe their label to be. Allow them to take off the label and look at it.

➥ Ask these questions:

> How did it feel to be labeled and treated according to the label?
> How did it feel to have to figure out what others thought?
> Do you see any similarities between this game and gossip? If so, what are they?
> Does gossip have to be false to be gossip? Is passing on the truth about someone gossiping?
> Can you gossip nicely about someone? Why, or why not?

WHAT WOULD YOU DO?
(15 minutes)

➠ Form small groups of three to six persons and distribute the situation cards and Bibles. (See FYI.)

➠ Ask each group to research these Scriptures:

✝ **Matthew 15:10-20**
✝ **2 Corinthians 12:19-20**
✝ **James 3:1-12**

➠ Using the Scriptures, participants will discuss the dilemmas, suggest a solution, and prepare to defend their solution to the group. Ask each group to report to the large group.

➠ Have the participants consider these questions as they work on their solutions:

How do you decide when to talk and when to keep quiet?
When is power the underlying issue, rather than a person's safety or the "greater good"?

* One day just before first period, Alan noticed that his good friend Jake had a bottle of whiskey hidden in his locker and that he took a drink every chance he got. When Jake noticed that Alan saw him drinking, he begged him not to tell anyone. Jake promised that he was only holding it for a friend and that he really did not have a problem. The next afternoon in geometry class Jake made a cruel remark about Alan's new haircut, and the whole class laughed. To get Jake back after class, Alan told some girls that Jake was a drunk and mentioned the bottle in the locker.

---

* Rebecca was excited about her date with Sam. They were going to the dance on Friday. Rebecca's brother Gil had heard that Sam kept a stash of marijuana in his car and was afraid for her. Gil knew that if he told Rebecca about the grass, she would not go to the dance with Sam. But he also knew that she would tell everyone and really trash Sam's reputation. Gil could not decide if he should tell his sister what he had heard on the basis of rumor.

---

* Suzanne really wanted the cheerleading spot that had come open this fall. Her only real competition was Ruth. The day before the tryouts Suzanne overheard some of her girlfriends talking loudly in the lunchroom about Ruth. They were saying that Ruth was really "loose" sexually with boys. In particular, they were accusing her of sleeping with Roy, who happened to be a friend of Suzanne's. Suzanne knew for a fact that the stories they were telling about Ruth were false, but she also knew that the rumors would help her get elected to the cheerleading squad.

ZACCHAEUS' STORY

Zacchaeus was a short man who had to climb a tree to get a glimpse of Jesus when he came through Jericho. But Jesus, who was especially sensitive to people who were left out for any reason, saw him in the tree. Jesus called to Zacchaeus to come down and take him to his home. The people whispered among themselves and said of Zacchaeus, "This man is a sinner and a tax collector!" Jesus knew they were whispering about Zacchaeus and himself as well saying, "What kind of man eats with sinners?"

Jesus went to Zacchaeus' home and ate and talked with him. The Bible does not say what the two men talked about, but it does say that Zacchaeus was a changed man. He offered to give back half of his goods and to give back four times any money that he might have stolen.

WHAT IS GOSSIP? (10 minutes)

Older Youth

➡ On a chalkboard or on newsprint draw a chart, listing down the left side the characters (mentioned or implied) from the situations just discussed: Ty, Denny, Alan, Jake, classmates, Rebecca, Gil, Sam, Suzanne, Ruth, girlfriends, Roy, other cheerleaders.

➡ Ask the group members to list some of the criteria they used for deciding what was gossip in their discussions (Who is helped? Who is hurt? What is the effect on me? What is the effect on others? How do I know what's true?).

➡ Use abbreviations for these criteria and add them to the chart across the top as column headings. Discuss with the group members the consequences of gossiping as you record their observations on the chart.

➡ Use these categories of questions to help:

 * *Observation:* Who said what about whom? How do you establish the truth of what is said?
 * *Interpretation:* How can we understand what was said? From how many points of view can we consider this information? What are the possible consequences of different decisions, based on those points of view?
 * *Application:* How can you take these various points of view or ways of looking at an issue and use them in another situation?

Younger Youth

➡ On a chalkboard or on newsprint list the characters (mentioned or implied) from the situations discussed: Ty, Denny, Alan, Jake, classmates, Rebecca, Gil, Sam, Suzanne, Ruth, girlfriends, Roy, other cheerleaders.

➡ Form three or four small groups and ask each small group to select three or four different characters. Have them answer the following questions about those characters:

> What was said about the person by others?
> Did you think it was fair? Why, or why not?
> If everybody believed the gossip, what different things could happen to that character?
> If nobody believed the gossip, what might have happened to the characters?
> Was there a character you didn't like? Why?
> Was it fun to gossip about any of the characters? Is there any reason for that gossip to be okay? Why?
> How do you think you would feel in the place of the person who was gossiped about? Why?

CREATE A SKIT (20 Minutes)

➥ Read aloud **Luke 19:1-10** about Zacchaeus or read the paraphrase. (See FYI, page 50.) Then discuss the following questions:

> What did the people of Jericho say about Zacchaeus?
>
> Why do you think this might be considered gossip?
>
> What effect might the people's words have had on Zacchaeus?
>
> How did Jesus respond to the whispered words of the townspeople?
>
> What do you notice about the way Jesus treated people who spoke ill of someone?
>
> What principle might we draw from this about the way we hear gossip?
>
> Why do you think Jesus did not listen seriously to gossip? What did Jesus know, which we forget, about people?

➥ Form small groups of four to six persons. Using the principles learned so far, ask the group members to create two skits about one situation they have encountered or know about.

➥ The skit will have two endings. The first ending should illustrate someone who does not believe in people the way that Jesus does. The second ending should illustrate someone who believes in people the way in which Jesus does.

WORSHIP

Gather in a circle. Give everyone paper and a pencil.

Affirm one another. Gossip is usually known as saying negative or damaging things about another person. After a moment of silence, ask each person to write his or her name on the paper and pass it to the right. That new person should write at least one positive thing about the person named on the paper, fold the paper down, and pass it to the right. The paper should be passed around the circle until it reaches the "owner."

Read aloud James 3:1-12 followed by a moment of silence. Ask the group to remain silent and consider the following questions:

* Who are the people that I may have wronged by gossip? Think of at least two or three persons.

* What are the things that are positive about these persons? How does God see them?

* What are you willing to do to stop gossip among your friends?

Sing "We Are One in the Spirit" (No. 975, *Supplement to The Book of Hymns: Supplemental Worship Resource II*).

What Makes Him or Her So Popular?

by Natalie L. Woods

PURPOSE:

To help youth recognize some of the myths and realities concerning attractiveness and popularity and to help them sort through how they feel about themselves as potential dates.

PREPARATION

➡ Provide several sheets of newsprint, markers, tape, Bibles, commentaries for Mark and First Corinthians, and at least one copy of *The United Methodist Hymnal*.

➡ If possible, provide video equipment for taping and playing back the dramatization of **1 Corinthians 13** (see page 55).

FOR YOUR INFORMATION

INHERITED TRAITS

How do you define "inherited traits"? We hear, "I have my mother's sense of humor"; I got my dad's temper"; I inherited the Hynson family stubbornness." Are these traits really inherited or are they learned? And if they are learned (or deeply ingrained) can they be unlearned or changed to something better? What do you think?

WHAT MAKES POPULAR PEOPLE POPULAR? (15 minutes)

➡ Tape several sheets of newsprint to the walls.

➡ Have the group members name popular groups of people from school and people in the media: athletes (jocks), cheerleaders, TV/movie/music stars. You may want to limit the categories.

➡ List each group across the top of a sheet of newsprint, creating columns. Form as many small groups as there are column headings. Designate a writer for each group.

➡ Ask the groups to brainstorm as many traits as they can think of that people in their category might possess. Then let each group have the opportunity to add to other groups' categories.

➡ Have the groups switch categories. Review the lists again and decide if each trait is a desired trait, an inherited trait, or an undesirable trait. (See FYI.)

WHAT IS BEING POPULAR?
(20 minutes)

➡ First have a general discussion of what it means to be popular. (See FYI.)

> What does being popular mean? (You always have someone to be with. You feel important. You are liked. Your opinion counts.)
>
> How is popularity like a two-edged sword? (It calls for decisions and actions. People can end up being treated as objects. It can cause people to forget values and faith.)

➡ Form age-level groups of three or four persons and provide newsprint and a marker for each group.

➡ The small groups will create two popular teen profiles by first drawing the outline of a body on the newsprint. Then ask the group members to think about two specific (and unnamed) popular persons at school, one male and one female. (Members of the youth group are not eligible.)

➡ Next have the participants fill in the silhouettes using words or symbols that describe those popular persons (smart, wears designer jeans and sneakers, tough, student body president, and so on).

➡ Have each group tape their silhouettes to a wall as the group explains their popular teen profiles. Discuss the profiles, noticing also any unique gender issues, by asking:

> What popularity traits appear most often?
>
> How do the profiles differ?
>
> Are any of the traits harmful to that person or to others? Give reasons for your answer.
>
> What are some traits that unpopular people often wish they possessed? Why, do you think?
>
> What are some good things about being popular? Why?
>
> What are some bad things about being popular? Why?
>
> What feelings do unpopular people have toward popular people? Why, do you think?
>
> How do these traits and feelings translate into the qualities you look for in a potential date?
>
> What traits do you want in a date? do you offer?

BEING POPULAR

Popularity is the state of being well liked and well-known. It's about being accepted.

Popularity is something that people give to other people. Popularity is not something that is naturally yours. Sometimes people are popular because they are nice and fun to be around. Sometimes people are popular because they have lots of money, a nice car, fashionable or expensive clothes, or because they do interesting or exciting things.

Popularity, in itself, is neither good nor bad. It is how the popular person, or people around the popular person, act or talk that makes the difference.

A MODEL FOR POPULARITY

Self-esteem plays a major part in how people view themselves. Often we have to be able to identify good things in ourselves that the casual observer might not see or notice. By the same token, we need to find positive qualities that are hidden in others and encourage them to grow in those qualities.

One way you can give yourself a self-esteem boost is to list the different (healthy) ways you strive to feel important and compare them to the reasons you believe that God truly values you. Look up **Genesis 1:26-31**; **John 3:16-17**; and **Romans 5:6-8** for biblical boosts.

Consider investing thirty minutes in an activity for your own growth, health, and well-being, such as practicing giving sincere compliments or meeting with your Christian friends to identify one another's gifts.

Another idea is to list the groups you would like to belong to. Specify which needs each group would fill for you. Now answer these questions: What price would you pay to belong to that group, if any? How would your self-esteem benefit from belonging to that group?

The bottom line is that popularity is bestowed on a person by a group. The other side of that coin is that popularity usually has a price. The question is, Is it a price you want to pay?

JESUS: A MODEL FOR POPULARITY? (15-18 minutes)

Older Youth

➡ Divide into small groups of three or four persons. Provide a Bible and a commentary on Mark, newsprint, and a marker for each group.

➡ On one sheet of newsprint the participants are to list things Jesus did or said that helped to make him popular (raising Lazarus from the dead, turning the water into wine, feeding people, and so on).

➡ Ask the participants to read **Mark 2:1–3:6** or assign portions to each small group so that the whole group divides the passage. Logical divisions are **Mark 2:1-12, 2:13-17, 2:18-22, 2:23-28,** and **3:1-6**.

➡ Have the group members study this passage to discover what Jesus did that made him both popular and unpopular (even at the same time, depending on the point of view!). Then discuss "A Model for Popularity." (See FYI.)

> What are some other things that Jesus did that he probably would not have done if all he wanted was to be popular?
> How could a goal of popularity have changed this passage? other parts of Jesus' ministry?

➡ Have the group members take turns retelling this story as a fictional account of Jesus' quest for popularity above all else. Take the story as far as it will go. Discuss these questions:

> How does the story change when the focus is popularity and not love?
> What did Jesus do that was not popular?
> Jesus called a group of disciples to work with him, but it was not an issue of popularity. What controls your life: the need for popularity, loyalty to Jesus Christ, or something else?

Younger Youth

➠ Assign **1 Corinthians 13**. Provide Bibles and a commentary on First Corinthians. Instruct the youth to read through the chapter, look at the commentary, and discuss any verses they do not understand.

➠ Then ask for a volunteer who can read the chapter with voice emphasis and pauses, helping to create a biblical drama. The other group members will recreate the story in pantomime as it is read aloud. (Movements can be extravagant.) Invite the actors to also create "freeze" poses to highlight the reading.

➠ If possible, videotape the performance so that the group members can view themselves. Then discuss the following questions:

> What impact does love have on popularity?
> What traits mentioned in **1 Corinthians 13** are easy to do? Which are hard? Why?
> How do these traits tie in to popularity?

WORSHIP

Begin with individual prayer. Allow the group members the opportunity to pray silently and out loud with petitions to God for traits that would be popular with God. For a visual prayer, instruct the youth to pantomime or act out the trait being prayed for.

Pray together. Have the group repeat after a leader a "Prayer for a New Heart" (No. 392 in *The United Methodist Hymnal*).

Share joys and concerns. Allow youth an opportunity to express joys and concerns for themselves and their friends. Take time to have volunteers talk about how to be yourself and how to help others to be who they are.

Offer a challenge. Challenge the youth to think about who they really are in relation to the development of their own character, personality, and abilities. Observe a few minutes of silence so that the youth will have a chance to reflect on the challenge issued and how they will respond.

Sing or say a hymn. Close with "On Eagle's Wings" (No. 143 in the *Hymnal*).

SOCIAL

How Do I Know What's Right?

by David F. White

PURPOSE:

To help youth understand the process of decision-making, to assess how they determine right from wrong, to think through how they define and identify what is authoritative for them, and to examine this process in the context of their faith.

PREPARATION

➡ Provide index cards, Bibles, Bible dictionaries, commentaries, pencils, paper, and copies of the *Discipline* and *The United Methodist Hymnal*.

➡ Bring taped instrumental music and a cassette player.

FOR YOUR INFORMATION

WESLEY'S QUADRILATERAL

John Wesley, the founder of Methodism, called himself "a man of one Book," referring to his belief and trust in the Bible. But even John Wesley thought it was important for a person to use all four ways of knowing to make decisions about life: Scripture, tradition, reason, and experience. For Methodists these four factors have always been important filters in making decisions.

Scripture is the central authority, but it is not static. God speaks in new ways in new times to persons through the timeless words of Scripture. The Bible does not mean just one thing for everyone,

BUZZ BOWL (15-20 minutes)

➡ Ask two youth to discuss a controversial topic from conflicting viewpoints. Send them to a separate room for five minutes to decide on the topic (suggestions: censoring violence on TV, metal detectors in schools, and so on).

➡ While the two group members are out of hearing range, form four smaller groups and ask them to listen to and take notes on arguments from Scripture, tradition, reason, and experience. (See the FYI information on "Wesley's Quadrilateral.")

➡ Bring back the two buzz bowlers who've been separated from the group. Take about seven or eight minutes for the dialogue.

➡ After the discussion, quickly review the parts of the Quadrilateral for the discussants, and then talk about the following questions:

> To what sources of authority for decisions did the discussants appeal the most? the least?
> Why do you think these sources were popular or less popular? When were Scripture and tradition most often used?

When were reason and experience most often used?
When you make decisions, whom or what do you
turn to most frequently for help?
What role do parents play? What role do friends play?

PRACTICE MAKING DECISIONS (10-15 minutes)

➡ Photocopy the situations and attach them to the index cards. (See FYI.)

➡ Form up to four small groups. Give each group a Bible and a Bible dictionary, a *Discipline*, paper and pencils, and a set of the situation index cards.

➡ Ask each group to summarize briefly their findings on these situations using the four sources of reason, tradition, Scripture, and experience. Have the small groups report back to the whole group, and then discuss the following questions:

What difficulties did you have in finding what each of
the four sources has to say?
How does using these sources make decision-making
easier? more difficult?
Do all these sources always speak clearly to each situation? Give reasons for your answer.
How is this way of making decisions different from
how you commonly make decisions?

because persons experience God and God's revelation through Scripture in a variety of ways.

Tradition refers to the history and teachings of the church in particular. What have our forebears in the faith done? What precedent have they established? How does that history or tradition apply today?

Reason is rooted in the scientific influence of the community as well as in the human capacity to weigh alternatives against the values, rules, and boundaries of the community. What has conventional wisdom revealed? What have we been able to prove or demonstrate empirically? What does our common sense tell us?

Experience of one's own or of others gives authority to past learnings that have general applications. What happened before in a similar situation? What options were available? What consequences could be observed from past experience?

SITUATIONS

*Randy is the youth group president. His friend George has asked him to come to a particular youth camp in the summer with the other youth. George has AIDS and has been shunned by other teens at school and in his neighborhood. George admits that while the risk is extremely slight of anyone else becoming infected, he is aware that some youth and parents will be afraid. Randy has agreed to bring the request before the youth council for consideration. You are the youth council. Using Scripture, reason, tradition, and experience, what decision would you offer?

*Fred is a student at Central High School and is confused about what career to pursue. John is his career counselor and wants to give him guidance that is truly Christian. From Scripture, reason, tradition, and experience, what guidance should John give to Fred?

*Flo is a friend of Shari's who has come to her for advice. Flo is involved in a group of youth who smoke marijuana and are pressuring Flo to do it too. Flo says that they reason that "God made it and it is a natural plant—so why not enjoy it?" Shari wants to give Flo advice that is truly Christian. What can she offer her from tradition, reason, experience, and Scripture?

*Betty goes to school each day in an urban area where she passes Ginny, a homeless person who sleeps in the doorway of a bank. For the past few days Ginny has asked Betty for money for food. Some friends warn her against getting involved. Betty has not been able to sleep some nights for thinking about Ginny. Using the sources of Scripture, reason, tradition, and experience, what would you be able to suggest to Betty?

DECISION BY COMMITTEE BIBLE STUDY (10-15 minutes)

➧ Divide into age-level groups and assign the following Scriptures to each group. Provide commentaries.

- ✞ **Joshua 2:1-15** (Rahab)
- ✞ **Judges 4:4-11** (Deborah)
- ✞ **Matthew 26:6-13** (woman with the ointment)
- ✞ **Luke 10:38-42** (Mary of Bethany)

Older Youth

➧ For each of the four passages, choose one person to represent the main character.

➧ Read the first passage aloud for the entire group. Ask the person representing the main character to identify the decision she is making in the passage.

➧ Ask the rest of the group members to use the Scripture passage and their imagination to determine what influences might be causing conflict. These influences might include friends, God, Scripture, tradition, personal desires, law, or personal danger.

➧ The group members should try to convince the main character of their point of view. Engage the other participants and the main character in a discussion about the decision at hand. Call time after everyone has had a chance to speak. Move to the next character.

➧ Discuss these questions:

> Are there ever times when you should give priority to one source of authority or another? When?
> When do you think the Scriptures might be more important than the other sources of tradition, reason, and experience?
> Are there ever times when reason or experience is more important than Scripture in making decisions? When? Why?

Younger Youth

➠ Ask the youth to gather in four small groups. Assign each group a Scripture passage to roleplay.

➠ The roleplay should have a twist, however. In each case the youth should roleplay the passage imagining that the characters also had friends who used negative peer pressure to influence them.

➠ After acting out how the character made her decision, discuss the following questions:

> Do you think these characters had the influence of peer pressure to deal with?
> What other influences might have made it hard to do God's will?
> What makes it hard for you to do God's will?

GUIDED IMAGERY (5 minutes)

➠ Ask the group members to get comfortable, take a few deep breaths, and close their eyes. Play soft music during this exercise to create a meditative mood.

➠ Ask them to see in their mind's eye a place where they can feel comfortable—a fireplace hearth, a grassy field, for example—and to picture a decision they currently face.

➠ Suggest that the participants listen to the conflicting voices surrounding that decision and to picture a wise person. Some will want to picture Jesus as their wisdom figure. Ask them to listen in their hearts to what the wise figure says about their decision.

➠ Debrief this exercise by forming pairs to talk over (as they feel comfortable) their situation, the decisions they face, and how their wisdom figure helps.

WORSHIP

Open with prayer. "O God, our paths sometimes seem dark. Give us the light of wisdom that comes from Scripture, tradition, reason, and experience. Give us a sense of your presence and touch our hearts with a love of life that spills over to others and to you. Amen."

Offer a verbal symbol of a current decision. Ask the participants to name or describe a symbol of a decision that they are in the midst of making.

Say the litany responsively.
LEADER: Open our eyes that we may see life and love from you, O God,
ALL: in the Scriptures.
LEADER: Open our ears that we may hear the voices of how you touched our friends, family, and forebears,
ALL: in the traditions.
LEADER: Help us taste your goodness all around us as we find you speaking to us,
ALL: in our experience of life.
LEADER: And may we feel you in our minds and in our hearts as we search for you,
ALL: in our reason. Draw us near to you in peace that we may glorify you. Amen.

Sing "Breathe on Me, Breath of God" (No. 420 in *The United Methodist Hymnal*).

Homophobia: Who is My Neighbor?

by Lynn L. Euzenas

PURPOSE:

To help sensitize youth to the issue of homophobia, assist them in developing a caring Christian response to the issue, and provide a sensitive Christian environment in which to discuss the relationship of the church to gay and lesbian persons.

PREPARATION

Note: This program is not about the rightness or wrongness of homosexuality. It is about the fear of (and behavior toward) persons who are homosexual, and it deserves open, careful preparation.

➡ Carefully review the FYI section before planning the session.

➡ Invite a pastor or counselor who is sensitive to and experienced in dealing with homophobia to be present to share leadership of this program. Work with him or her or other leaders of the church on the optional panel discussion.

➡ Obtain several copies of the *Book of Discipline*, *The United Methodist Hymnal*, and a Bible, preferably one with textual notes, for each participant. Gather commentaries on the texts, a box, a bowl of water, and towels.

➡ Provide paper and pencils for everyone.

FOR YOUR INFORMATION

WHAT IS HOMOPHOBIA?

Homophobia is defined as an irrational fear of a person who is lesbian or gay. We often see or hear this fear exhibited in unkind jokes, rejection, exclusion, or violence against such persons.

Disagreement with and disapproval of homosexuality are not necessarily homophobic. Likewise, though we may not consider ourselves homophobic or prejudiced

WHAT IS HOMOPHOBIA? (5-8 minutes)

➡ Review the definition and commentary on homophobia. (See FYI.) Allow time for discussion of what homophobia is (not for discussing homosexuality).

WHAT DOES THE CHURCH SAY? (15 minutes)

➡ Read aloud Paragraph 71 F (pages 91–92; especially the last paragraph of this section) and Paragraph 71 G (page 92) from the *Book of Discipline*.

➡ Form small groups of two or three persons and ask them to write a reverse paraphrase of the last paragraph of section 71 F and of section 71 G. Discuss what the reverse wording says about these issues (see the top of page 61):

* the worth of homosexual persons
* homosexuals' relationship to the church
* the practice of homosexuality
* the availability of God's grace
* the church's commitment to ministry
* the rights of gay and lesbian persons
* the climate of violence against homosexual persons

➠ Then discuss these questions:

Which version affirms the worth of all persons?
Which version limits God's grace?
Which version condones the practice of homosexuality?
Which version sounds homophobic?
Which version is the official stance of United Methodists?
What do you think the stance of the church should be on homophobia (not homosexuality)?

WHO IS MY NEIGHBOR?
(15 minutes)

➠ Introduce the Bible study by reading or summarizing the commentary on this section. (See FYI.)

➠ Form teams of three or four persons and ask each team to read **Genesis 19:1-11; Ezekiel 16:49-50**; and one of the following passages:

✝ **Matthew 22:34-40** (Love your neighbor.)
✝ **Luke 7:36-50** (Jesus is the perfect host.)
✝ **John 15:12-17** (Love one another.)
✝ **1 Peter 4:8** (Love covers a multitude of sins.)
✝ **1 John 4:16-21** (Perfect love casts out fear.)

➠ Have the teams read and compare what the Bible says about the way the men of Sodom acted and about how we should treat our neighbors, both in what we offer and in what we receive from them. Then discuss answers to the following questions:

What contrasts do you see?
What do the passages say about fear? about love? about responsibility? about hospitality?
Why do you think Jesus never specifically talked about homosexuality or about fearing persons who are homosexual?

against homosexual persons, if we feel uncomfortable or repulsed by talking with or about gay or lesbian persons, we are experiencing our own form of homophobia.

As Christians, homophobia affects us just as racism, sexism, or anti-Semitism does: It intentionally separates us from others because of fear, dislike, hatred, or difference. Fearing what we do not know or understand is not unusual. Honest dialogue, while not requiring agreement, promotes respect and casts out fear.

WHO IS MY NEIGHBOR?

Genesis 19:1-11 provides a useful study on the issue of homophobia because the condemnation of homosexality is in question and because it deals with the issue of hospitality. **Genesis 19** is often cited to label the sin of Sodom as homosexuality.

An alternate exegesis of this passage holds that the sin of Sodom is identified in **Ezekiel 16:49-50** as pride, arrogant treatment of others, gluttony, and lack of care and concern for the poor and needy.

The men of Sodom are characterized as vicious and fearsome and are dealt with harshly by God because of it. While they certainly presented a threat of violence, we cannot assume all the people of Sodom were alike. All the righteous of the city were to be spared (**Genesis 18:20-33**).

The New Testament passages deal with hospitality. Jesus is silent on the subject of homosexuality, although he was doubtless aware of passages that refer to it as an abomination (**Leviticus 18:22** and **20:13**, for example). He is clear about the treatment of our neighbors, even those we may feel we have every right to despise. Jesus ate with sinners, spoke to a Samaritan woman, called a tax collector to be a disciple, and preached about love for "the least."

Note: It is important when reading the biblical texts that deal with homosexuality to deal with the issue of proof-texting. Often texts such as those from Leviticus are removed from the context of the book in order to prove a point, while other texts in the same book are no longer applied to daily living; for example, the prohibition against eating swine (**Leviticus 11:7-8**), or the instructions that anyone who maims another human being should in turn be maimed (**Leviticus 24:19**). Urge investigation that keeps a passage in its context and that is open to both traditional and alternative interpretation.

If you have time, discuss with the group why these sample passages are not used today, while the prohibition against homosexual behavior is used.

WALKING IN ANOTHER'S SHOES

Often the only image of a gay or lesbian person which we have is a caricature or stereotyped one that is often negative and hurtful. Gay and lesbian persons come from all walks of life. Without realizing it, we may know persons who are gay or lesbian but who cannot share that part of themselves due to fear for their relationship, job, housing, and safety.

As Christians, getting beyond stereotypes can help us to understand that homosexual people like to have friends, a good job, go to church, party, laugh, and feel joy and pain just like everyone else. We also know that Christians have strong opinions concerning homo-

WALKING IN ANOTHER'S SHOES
(10-15 minutes)
➟ Divide into age-level groups.

Older Youth
➟ Review the introductory remarks and read or paraphrase that information for the group. (See FYI.)

➟ Discuss these questions. If time permits, either discuss or do the roleplay suggestions for younger youth.

> How could getting beyond the stereotypes help us to lessen our fear of homosexual persons?
> How would you respond if you discovered that someone you respect is a gay or lesbian person?
> How would you treat your gay or lesbian neighbor?
> How do you think Jesus would treat gay or lesbian people?

Younger Youth
➟ Roleplay the following situations, taking time for discussion after the completion of all the roleplays.

* Your best friend calls and says he would like to talk to you in private. He then confides in you that he thinks he is gay. What do you do and say? (Thinking so and being so are not necessarily the same.)

* You are walking home with some friends after going to the movies and a group of boys follows you, frightening you and calling you derogatory names, suggesting that you are a homosexual. You are not. How do you feel after such an experience?

* You are having lunch at school and you know that one of the people at the table is a lesbian. Some at the table start telling nasty jokes about gay and lesbian persons and laughing. As a Christian, what do you do? should you do?

WHAT YOU CAN DO NOW
(5 minutes)

➠ Review these strategies that address homophobia:

* Be aware that homophobia is hurtful. Resolve to keep from telling jokes or using names that are hurtful to others.

* Try walking in another person's shoes. Can you relate to the loneliness and difficulty of being afraid to be who you fully are?

OPTIONAL: HAVE A PANEL DISCUSSION (30-60 minutes)

➠ Invite a guest speaker from an organization like PFLAG: Parents and Friends of Lesbians and Gays, or Affirmation: United Methodists for Gay, Lesbian, and Bisexual Concerns to talk to the group. Listen to what it is like to be a gay or lesbian person, or the parent or friend of a person who is gay. Have an honest discussion with the group about their feelings concerning what is heard.

sexuality. Disagreeing with or disapproving of homosexuality should not lead to fear.

WORSHIP

Gather in a large circle around a table with a bowl of water, several clean towels, and a box on the table.

Offer confession. Participants will write on slips of paper a confession of times they have not loved their neighbor, have felt unfounded hatred for others, or have acted thoughtlessly towards persons who are different from them. The papers do not need to be signed. Hold them for later.

Pray together. "Holy God, healer of all peoples, receive these statements of our failings, and bring us to forgiveness. Heal our wounds and the wounds we cause others to have, directly or indirectly. Place in us a spirit of love, so that we may love and live in sisterhood and brotherhood with all persons, no matter how different they may seem to us. Help us, as your church, to be more loving toward persons who are gay or lesbian. Help us, as your people, to open our hearts and work to eradicate prejudice and fear in all that we do. In Jesus' name. Amen."
(*Place the papers in the box.*)

Receive the pardon. Participants will come forward (several at a time), and experience the cleansing power of God's loving and forgiving presence. They will dip their hands in the bowl and wash them and may wash another's hands.

Sing or say "Spirit of the Living God" (No. 393 in *The United Methodist Hymnal*).

Get On Line!

Get in touch with the issues that make growing up so difficult for 11- to 14-year-olds. Get a youth study plan for dealing with the negative influences in young lives. Get *On Line With Jesus Christ!*

On Line With Jesus Christ is a life skills program for grades 7–9 that will help youth:
◆ develop the convictions of faith necessary in today's culture
◆ learn and practice essential life skills, like communication, goal setting and decision making
◆ become more active followers of Jesus Christ
◆ build healthy relationships

Teachers of *On Line* are prepared to present this 36-week program through a one-day training session. Resources included in this Christian education package are:
◆ One-day Leadership Training Seminar for two adult leaders
◆ Leader's Guide with Audiocassettes, CA4-475287
◆ 8 Sets of Student Journals (3 Journals per set), CA4-475538
◆ 8 Sets of Parent Newsletters (6 Newsletters per set), CA4-475864
◆ *Jesus of Nazareth* VHS Video, CA4-475309

To order *On Line With Jesus Christ* or for more information, call Cokesbury at 1-800-672-1789.

Cokesbury
Books ● Bibles ● Church Resources

CALL OR VISIT YOUR COKESBURY STORE
ORDER FROM YOUR COKESBURY SERVICE CENTER
201 Eighth Avenue South ● P.O. Box 801
Nashville, TN 37202-0801

ORDER TOLL FREE: 1-800-672-1789

FAX ANYTIME: 1-800-445-8189

USE YOUR COKESBURY ACCOUNT, DISCOVER, VISA, AMERICAN EXPRESS, OR MASTERCARD.

TDD/TT TOLL-FREE SERVICE: 1-800-227-4091 (Telecommunications Device for the Deaf/Telex Telephone)

● ● ●

Satisfaction Guaranteed! Please add your state's sales tax. Prices subject to change without notice. Shipping and handling extra.

SPIRITUAL ISSUES

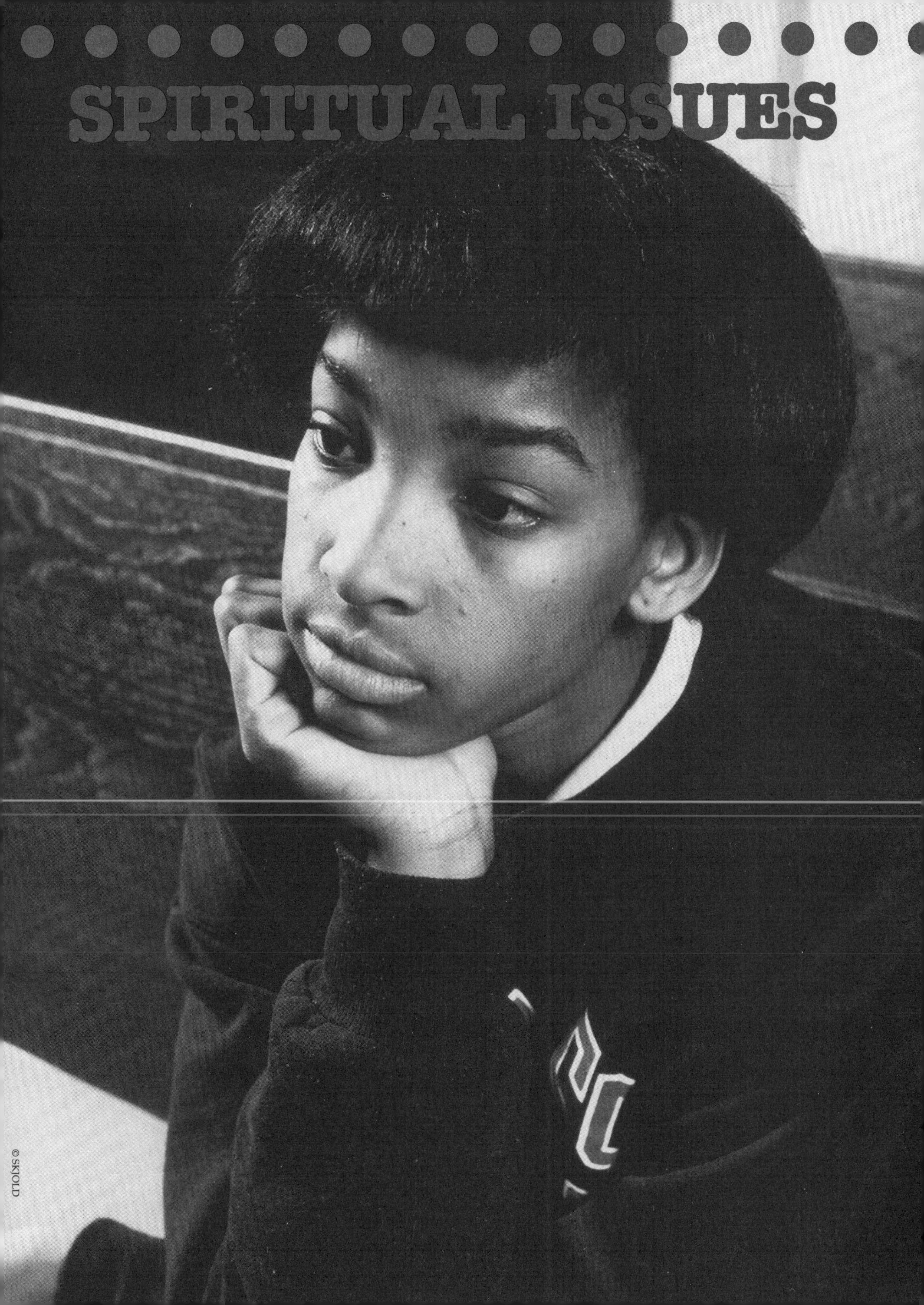

SPIRITUAL

Suffering: How Long, O Lord?

by A. Okechukwu Ogbonnaya

▶ PURPOSE:

To help youth look at suffering and God's place in human suffering and to explore the impact of suffering on faith and of faith on suffering.

▶ PREPARATION

➠ Have on hand chalk and a chalkboard or newsprint and markers, crayons, and other (optional) supplies for a mural.

➠ Have a Bible and a copy of *The United Methodist Hymnal* for each participant and commentaries for the Scriptures.

➠ Invite a guest speaker to converse with the group about his or her own experience of suffering. He or she should be prepared to talk positively about the role of faith in the midst of that suffering. Suggest ahead of time that group members develop a list of questions. **You may also do this in an extended or second session.**

FOR YOUR INFORMATION

THE PROBLEM OF JOB: GOD AND SUFFERING

The following dialogue, based on the context of Job's suffering, highlights some of the attitudes that various persons may have as they relate to someone who suffers. Job had three friends named Eliphaz, Bildad, and Zophar. Each had a specific idea about suffering.

Job's response to each one reflects his understanding of the issue from the perspective of the sufferer. It shows his faith and his struggle with the seeming absence of God in the face of his trials.

JOB: Why am I alive? I feel like dying. God is persecuting me for

THE PROBLEM OF JOB (10 minutes)

➠ Ask for volunteers to present the dramatic reading about Job and his friends. (See FYI.)

➠ After the drama talk about the problem of Job and his friends.

> What are the things that impressed you most in the conversation? Why?
> What are some words, statements, or attitudes that "turned you off"? Why?
> Have you ever felt like Job? When and why?
> Do you think his experience is like anyone else's? Why, or why not?

THE GREAT DEBATE (15 minutes)

➡ Form two teams (or multiples of two in a large group). One team will argue for the truthfulness of the following statements and the other for the falsity of the statements. You could have five teams, one for each of the statements. The purpose of the debate is to raise ideas, not to force persons to adopt a particular point of view.

➡ Select someone to record on newsprint or the chalkboard the main points made by each team.

➡ Debate these statements:

* Good things happen to good people and bad things happen to bad people.
* If someone is suffering, he or she must be guilty of some sin.
* Persons suffer only because of a lack of faith.
* Pain helps your faith grow.
* God "fits the back for the burden." If you have a heavy load of suffering, it's because God knows you can handle it.

➡ Debrief after the debates. Use these questions to get the conversation started:

> How convincing were the particular arguments? What points were the most controversial? the most agreeable?
>
> How do these statements about suffering square with your own experience?
>
> Do any of them help you endure suffering? Which ones? How?
>
> Do any of these statements make your suffering harder to handle? Which ones? Why?

nothing. What I am most afraid of has happened to me. I chose to serve God because I thought I would have peace, quiet, and rest, but all I got is pain.

ELIPHAZ: Think about it, Job. You have helped many people. But I am puzzled. I don't think innocent people suffer or righteous people are destroyed. God is always angry with the wicked; that's why they suffer. God is disciplining you. Don't despise the discipline of God. (Chapters 4–5)

JOB: I have done nothing to deserve this severity from God. You, my friends, should know that better than anyone else! I accuse God because I am desperate. I think about healing and the possibility that I might not be healed. Don't patronize me and don't ask me to be quiet. I have every reason to complain! (Chapters 6–7)

BILDAD: God is always right. If you really are righteous, God would have healed you and rescued you from your suffering. God does not reject good people. (Chapter 8)

JOB: I know that God is just and loves the righteous. My confusion comes from the fact that God seems to reject the blameless as well. God is treating me as someone who does not love God. Why? I hate my pain and so I complain. Does God enjoy my pain? (Chapters 9–10)

ZOPHAR: God can do whatever God wants. Those who devote themselves to God are always blessed. They have no need to fear; they are not ashamed; they are always secure and safe. (Chapter 11)

JOB: This doesn't make sense to me. I want to speak to God and argue my case directly. Even if it means being in greater danger, I'm going to have it out, honestly, with God. Let God explain why God has let me suffer so horribly! (Chapters 12–13)

The conversation continues in this vein throughout most of the rest of **Job**. The three friends are working out of a theological understanding of *retributive justice*, that is, that the good prosper and the wicked suffer and conversely, those who suffer must be wicked and those who seem blessed must be righteous. Job's experience indicates that this just is not true.

Eliphaz generally represents the case that God is always just, and so Job must be in error. He is going to help Job understand where he (Job) went wrong so Job can repent and regain his favor with God.

Bildad generally represents the point of view of ancient justice. God's actions are automatic within the context of retributive justice. God rewards persons based on their actions: good for good, bad for bad.

Zophar says, somewhat crudely, that persons are either good, wicked, or uninitiated and waiting to be guided toward one way or the other. God is rigid in God's dealings. He insists that Job's troubles are the result of his foolishness and that God can do nothing other than to punish him.

Job argues that there is more to it than his friends simplistically state. God is the creator of all things, and is in charge of all circumstances, including those in which evil befalls the righteous (echoed in **Matthew 5:45**).

EXAMINE THE SCRIPTURES (10-20 minutes)

Older Youth

➡ Read **Isaiah 43:1-4a** and **1 Corinthians 10:12-13**. Use the commentaries to help understand the passages, and then discuss these questions:

What do these passages say? What do you think they mean?
Do you see any connection between these passages? If so, what?
What are the promises in these references? Do you believe them? Why, or why not?
Have you had any experience in which these passages really helped you in a painful situation? Share what you wish.

➡ After the study and discussion, make a mural that depicts in contemporary ways what suffering through a "trial by fire" or a "trial by water" might be. Use butcher paper, markers, crayons, and other supplies.

➡ With the whole group, explain and discuss the murals.

Younger Youth

➡ Half the group will read **Daniel 3:1-18** and half will read **Daniel 3:19-30**. Consult a commentary for a better understanding of the passages.

➡ Retell the story in your own words to get a composite picture of the entire event. Then talk about these questions:

Why were Shadrach, Meshach, and Abednego in trouble with the king?
Do you think they were wise to risk such great danger and suffering for their position? Why, or why not?
They were not harmed at all. Do you think God protects everyone that way? Why, or why not?
Have you ever suffered or faced suffering for something that was very important to you? If so, did your faith help you?

➡ After the discussion, work on a liturgical dance or other artistic expression that represents how these three men faced their danger in the furnace. Select others to represent the other characters in the drama. You can also have dancers represent the fire. The dance can have "movements" that represent different stages of the event before, during, and after. Present the dance to the entire group.

PRESENT THE GUEST SPEAKER (15-20 minutes)

➠ Invite the guest to speak for a designated time and then to answer questions. You may also do this in an extended or second session. For the best use of the guest's time, have questions submitted ahead of time by the group members; but leave some time open for new insights and questions from participants.

➠ Allow persons to express any feelings they have related to the topic, but monitor how things are going. Comments and questions should be treated with compassion.

➠ If time permits, give the guest time to ask questions of the group members that may open their understanding of human suffering and God's place in the midst of it.

WORSHIP

Sing or say "Nobody Knows the Trouble I See" (No. 520 in *The United Methodist Hymnal*).

Pray together the prayer "For Overcoming Adversity" (No. 531 in the *Hymnal*). Those who wish may offer sentence prayers for those who are suffering. After each petition say together, "Lord, hear our prayer."
Continue with prayers of thanks for help in a time of adversity. After each thanksgiving, say together, "We give you thanks, O God."

Sing or say "I Want Jesus to Walk With Me" (No. 521 in the *Hymnal*).

Close with a benediction.

Does Doubt Make Me an Atheist?

by A. Okechukwu Ogbonnaya

PURPOSE:

To help youth understand what atheism is and how it differs from doubt or neglect of faith.

PREPARATION

➠ Have access to a chalkboard and chalk or newsprint and markers.
➠ Make point cards for each of the debate judges.
➠ Have a Bible and a copy of *The United Methodist Hymnal* for each person and commentaries on the Scripture passages.

FOR YOUR INFORMATION

MEET FIREBROOK, DIOGENES, AND WATERWAY

* FIREBROOK: Hi, Diogenes. Seen any spirits lately?
* DIOGENES: Spirit is always present in our hearts. You wouldn't know about that since you don't believe in God.
* FIREBROOK: Yeah, you're right. And the reason for my refusal to accept the existence of God is simple. There is nothing beyond the material structure of the world.
* DIOGENES: How can you be so sure that God does not exist?
* FIREBROOK: Because there's no scientific proof. Besides, if God is supposed to be so powerful and good, why is there so much suffering in the world?
* DIOGENES: Let me make sure

DISCOVER THE MEANING OF ATHEISM (5 minutes)

➠ Brainstorm personal understandings of atheism. Record suggested answers on the chalkboard or newsprint.

DEBATE YOUR BELIEFS (15 minutes)

➠ Form three debate teams. (Let the group members know that this is a way to enhance learning, not a competitive game.) Assign each team one of the positions on page 71.

➠ Each team will select a recorder, discuss their assigned position, develop their justification for the position, find two reasons against the other positions, and select two spokespersons to present their justification and offer the concluding remarks.

➠ Have the selected judges sit at a table and listen to the groups present their cases. They will score each group on a range of 5 (most convincing) to 1 (not at all convincing) and then will summarize aloud their findings:

* one unconvincing point made by each group
* one good point made by each group

Team 1. Atheists: State reasons for your refusal to believe in God. Remember that for the atheist the nonexistence of God is a certainty. God is not a part of your thinking.

Team 2. Theists: You believe in God; you have no doubt that there is a God. State some reasons for your belief in God. Remember that the existence of God cannot really be "proven," but the effect of the belief on a person can be demonstrated.

Team 3. Searchers: You believe, but you are currently struggling with your belief and sometimes you have serious doubts. State reasons or experiences that may have triggered your doubt or your crises of faith.

that I understand you. According to you, science can't prove that God exists, but suffering proves that God doesn't exist?

* FIREBROOK: That's it. Any "proof" you have is just in your mind or in your heart, as you might claim.

* DIOGENES: It seems to me that you have moved from the existence of God to the character of God. How can you speak of the character of something you think does not exist? How can you blame whom you say does not exist for the suffering of the world?

* FIREBROOK: I'm not blaming. I'm just explaining my argument. Here comes Windblow. She used to believe like you. Let's ask her.

* WINDBLOW: Are you two at it again? You debate too much. Besides, no one can ever really know whether there is a God.

* FIREBROOK: Windblow, you're just afraid to take a stand.

* WINDBLOW: Well, I can't defend what I don't know. I leave the two of you to waste your time.

   (Exit Windblow. Enter Waterway. Everyone exchanges greetings.)

* WATERWAY: I'm glad to see you both. I've been doing a lot of thinking about God. I mean the idea of God. Of a good God, really.

* DIOGENES: We were too. Our mutual friend here, Firebrook, is trying to convince me that there is no God.

* WATERWAY: That's good because I've decided there is no God. I struggle so much with my faith, I must be an atheist.

* DIOGENES: Why would you say such a thing? You were one of the strongest members of our youth group!

* WATERWAY: Too many bad things have happened to me in the past year. I believed in God and God let me down. I am not sure

that my faith in God is real.

* FIREBROOK: You see, he has come to know that the belief in God is nothing but a psychological crutch.

* DIOGENES: *(Looking at Firebrook and turning his gaze to Waterway)* Waterway, it seems to me that you are struggling with your faith in God.

* WATERWAY: Yes. I do not think I am a Christian anymore. How can I be a Christian and doubt the existence of God? I was in trouble, and I felt abandoned by God; and then I just wasn't so sure anymore.

* DIOGENES: You're not alone. Even the greatest persons of faith have had their moments of doubt. You are in good company— David, Jeremiah, Jesus, and even me, your good pal!

* WATERWAY: You mean you have doubted the existence of God?

* DIOGENES: You remember two years ago when I was in deep trouble? I didn't know what to think, and sometimes I was too down to pray or do anything. But my friends at church kept praying and after a while, I realized that God had been with me all the time.

* WATERWAY: Gee, I thought I had to do all this belief stuff by myself.

* FIREBROOK: Waterway, listen to Diogenes. You are no atheist; you're just confused. I will leave you two superstitious people.

* DIOGENES and WATERWAY: See you later.

A LOOK AT SCRIPTURE
(10-15 minutes)

➠ Form age-level groups.

Older Youth

➠ Read **Psalm 14:1-3**, research it in the commentary, and then discuss the following questions and points:

> Do you believe that atheists are fools? Why, or why not?
>
> Some have claimed that atheism leads to immorality. Even the psalmist connects atheism with moral corruption. What do you think?
>
> If the "heart" is the center of belief and unbelief, what connections, if any, do you see between unbelief and being a good person?

Younger Youth

➠ Read **Mark 11:20-24**, research it in the commentary, and discuss the following questions:

> What did Jesus do before he told his disciples to have faith in God?
>
> Do you think it is possible to believe in something as verse 23 suggests? Why, or why not?
>
> If someone does not believe, do you think God would treat him or her like the fig tree? Why, or why not?
>
> Do you think prayer can help us know God? If so, in what ways? If there were no God, would praying make any difference? Why, or why not?

MEET FIREBROOK, DIOGENES, AND WATERWAY (15-20 minutes)

➡ Ask for at least one team of three persons, plus Windblow, to act out the dialogue. (See FYI, pages 70–72.) If possible have the characters put their dialogue in their own words.

➡ If you want to use more than one team, decide where to switch in the dialogue. (You will need only one Windblow.)

➡ Set the scene as a hangout at the mall where the characters can meet.

➡ Other group members will listen to the dialogue and look for clues to the meanings of atheism, theism, and doubt. After the conversation, talk about these questions:

> What is Firebrook's position? Diogenes'? Waterway's? Windblow's? How do you know?
>
> Where do you find yourself in this dialogue? Which of the characters do you feel connected to and why?
>
> Have you ever felt like more than one of these characters at a time? If so, when? How?
>
> Do you think that having doubts about something means you don't, won't, or can't ever believe? Why, or why not?
>
> Do you think that someone who actively disbelieves in God now will never believe? Why, or why not?
>
> What is your level of belief now and how do you think you got there?

WORSHIP

Open with sentence prayers from members of the group.

Sing or say "I Will Trust in the Lord" (No. 464 in *The United Methodist Hymnal*).

Read Mark 9:14-24 and John 20:24-31.

Recite the Apostles' Creed, in the litany on page 41 in the *Hymnal.*

Share personal stories. Call on members of the group to share testimonies and struggles of faith. After every testimony the group should respond, "The Lord is God. Praise the name of God."

Sing or say "Through It All" (No. 507 in the *Hymnal*).

Living Your Own Faith

by Michael B. Walters

▶ PURPOSE:

To help youth live out and share their personal Christian beliefs without judging the beliefs of others.

▶ PREPARATION:

➡ Gather several Bibles, paper and pencils (no crayons or color markers), and tape.

➡ Make the "God Picture." (See FYI.)

➡ Provide pictures of Jesus by artists of various national origins and of different centuries. Check your church and local libraries.

➡ Acquaint yourself with the information about "being saved" in the FYI section.

➡ Have a copy of *The United Methodist Hymnal* for everyone.

FOR YOUR INFORMATION

THE GOD PICTURE

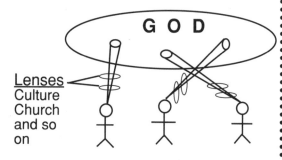

Draw a picture like the one shown above.

HAVE YOU BEEN SAVED?

"Have you been saved?" is a crucial question for our faith, but it often reflects a particular religious point of view. All Christians are saved by the crucifixion and resur-

YOUR PERSONAL PICTURE OF GOD (8-12 minutes)

➡ Give a piece of paper and a pencil to each person. Ask each participant to move to a place to work in private. Work in teams if your group is large.

➡ Explain that while we all know that God does not have a body as we do, and that God is a Spirit, we all have a personal image of who we pray to.

➡ Tell the participants they have five minutes to draw a picture that represents who they pray to and that everyone's drawing will be different. (This is not a contest!)

➡ Next, bring everyone together to guess who drew which picture and what it might mean. Have the "artist" explain what it represents to him or her.

THE BIG PICTURE (10 minutes)

➥ Put all the pictures up on a wall, close together.

➥ Ask if God is bigger than what these pictures show. Now put the "God Picture" up on the wall to suggest how each of us sees only a small part of God.

➥ Next, examine how denomination, culture, family, and friends serve as camera lenses through which we see God. Explain that these and other factors influence how we understand God. Divide into age-level groups to talk about these lenses.

Older Youth

How might these persons' understanding of God differ?
* a teen who can afford almost anything and one who can't
* a company president and a migrant worker
* an heiress to a fortune and her housekeeper
* a Roman Catholic and a United Methodist
* a teen who has experienced trauma and a teen who hasn't

If persons view God and their beliefs differently, does that mean someone is wrong? Give reasons for your answer.

Younger Youth

➥ Show the different pictures of Jesus. Talk about why they are not all alike. Then discuss these questions:

Why do you think the artists represented Jesus as a member of their own race or culture?

How might that similarity help persons understand Jesus and God?

Do you think there is one right or correct way to see Jesus and God? Give a reason for your answer.

rection of Jesus Christ. That act is a once and final act of God through Christ on our behalf, and no person can duplicate it or take it away.

"Have you been saved?" refers then to our own activity. This does not mean that we save ourselves; only God does that. But we have the choice to believe or not believe and to accept or not accept the blessings that are available to us through God's grace. We may further choose to act or not act according to a Christian set of beliefs and doctrine.

Some persons can remember the actual moment when they came to belief from unbelief; often that time is spoken of as the moment when they were "saved." Others have grown up in a different religious or faith environment and have always felt "saved." Neither of these experiences is better or worse than the other, and certainly there is no qualitative difference in persons because of those kinds of experiences. They reflect a bit of the diversity in the ways persons experience God and the Christian faith. Diverse persons becoming unified in God's love is one of the treasures of our faith.

Sometimes the language of "being saved" is used very much in earnest and expresses an interest in a person's relationship with Christ. On other occasions it can be used to encourage, coax, cajole, or pester a person to accept a particular belief in a particular way. Some persons object to that kind of encounter and feel that it discounts their own beliefs and ways of believing.

When any of us insist that another person believe exactly as someone else does or suggest that there is only one way to be "saved" (referring to our act, not God's), we risk diminishing a brother or sister in the faith.

BASEBALL STORY

At the beginning of summer John met a new friend at the park. Sam and John both loved to watch and play baseball. They often would round up enough others for a game. The only interruption to this schedule was that John went to church every Sunday while his good friend Sam played baseball every Sunday morning.

Every week the conversation would be the same:

"Hey John, do you want to come play baseball with me? There's always room on the team for a good player like you."

"Naw, Sam, I've got church you know; maybe some other time, okay?"

One day, Sam came up to John and declared that he didn't want to be friends anymore. John was stunned.

"Why?" he asked.

Sam said, "Because you don't like me very much, that's why."

"What do you mean?" a stunned John replied.

Obviously hurt, Sam said, "John, you went to church every Sunday all summer long. I know that it must be real important to you, if you go every Sunday. So how come, when I have asked you to play ball with me every Sunday, not once have you ever asked me to go to church with you? I thought friends shared important things with each other."

HAVE YOU BEEN SAVED?
(8-10 minutes)

➡ Ask a volunteer to read aloud **Matthew 7:1-5** and **Luke 6:39-42** and then discuss these questions. (See FYI, "Have You Been Saved?" pages 74–75.)

> What do these Scriptures say about judgment?
> Can "judgment" refer to judging or evaluating the faith experience of others? Why, or why not?
> Is there only one way to be a Christian?
> Is there a right way and a wrong way to express or describe our faith? Explain your answers.
> Have you had someone insist that you believe a certain way? How did it feel? What did you think?
> Have you coaxed or argued with someone about believing a certain way? What was the result?

DISCUSSING THE FAITH
(10-15 minutes)

➡ Form age-level groups and work in small teams to complete the following scenes:

Older Youth

* Andrea says, "I don't think you can call God 'he.' God isn't male." What do you say?

* Rick says, "God doesn't listen to my prayers. If he did, my baby sister would not have died." What do you say?

Younger Youth

* Ty says, "I think God made everything in the world in six days." What do you say?

* Marcos says, "God is out there watching everything I do. I have to be good or he'll get me." What do you say?

SHARING THE FAITH
(7-10 minutes)
➡ Read aloud the "Baseball Story." (See FYI.)

Older Youth
➡ Break into pairs and discuss how you would share your faith with someone, and/or invite the person to church or a church function.

➡ Invite pairs to demonstrate before the group what they would say or do.

Younger Youth
➡ Discuss first the following questions about the story. Then take a few minutes to think of a couple of ways to invite someone to church or tell someone about your faith. Have each person describe what she or he would say and do.

> What are the major points of the story?
> Why do you think Sam invited John to play ball?
> Why do you think John never invited Sam to church?
> How might Sam have reacted to the invitation?
> What do you think someone would say to you if you invited him or her to church? Why do you think that?

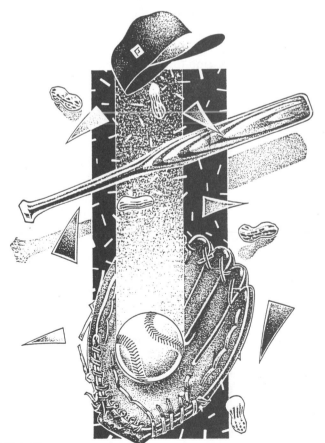

WORSHIP
Sing or say "Many Gifts, One Spirit" (No. 114 in *The United Methodist Hymnal*). Pay special attention to stanza two.

Ask for group concerns. Go around the group and ask if anyone would like to share something of what God is like to him or her.

Confess together. "God, forgive us when we have kept your name silent and when we have shouted your name so loudly we deafen others. In both cases the others cannot hear your sweet name; one because of silence, the other because of deafness.

"Forgive us and free us to proclaim your message of a joyful life through more than whispers or shouts; but in acts of love, words of friendship, and a life that has your joy overflowing. Amen."

Sing or say "Lead Me, Lord" (No. 473 in the *Hymnal*) as a benediction.

God as Object; God as Friend

by David F. White

PURPOSE:

To help youth recognize the difference between knowing God and knowing about God and learn how and why to cultivate a personal relationship with God.

PREPARATION

➡ Provide Bibles, paper and pencil, and an envelope for each person.

➡ Have on hand newsprint and markers or a chalkboard and chalk.

➡ Invite adults or older youth to lead small groups of youth in prayer, singing, dance, nature meditation, and so on. Brief them about their responsibilities for the meeting.

➡ Gather a candle, matches, copies of *The United Methodist Hymnal*, and other symbols for worship.

FOR YOUR INFORMATION

"KNOWING" AND "KNOWING ABOUT"

These two terms may not seem all that different, but they can be. Sometimes what we know about (or think we know about) someone or something is not really so, or is only a part of the picture. Sometimes what we truly know about someone leads us to a false assumption that we discover when we get better acquainted. Knowing—firsthand, personally—is usually more accurate, even intimate, than the secondhand knowing about.

DID I MISS A MEETING?

1. Ray's terrible temper seems to ruin his relationships. Two months ago Ray met Andrea, and he fell for

INTEREST HUNT (15 minutes)

➡ Give each person a sheet of paper and a pencil. Ask the participants to write on the sheet of paper ten things that are true about themselves, such as hobbies, interests, hopes, and so on. Allow one minute for this part.

➡ Collect the papers; then shuffle and redistribute them so that no one has his or her own description.

➡ The object is to identify each person by using only the information on the sheet. When the group members correctly identify the writer of a description, they should return the paper. Take five minutes or so.

➡ Have the group members pair up and interview each other briefly about things on the sheet or additional interesting facts. Then ask the following questions:

What was the most unusual fact discovered?

How was your person like or unlike the description?

Did the original descriptions fit the person who turned out to be the writer? Why? Why not?

How did the interview give you a fuller understanding of the other person than did his or her list?

What is the difference between knowing about someone and knowing someone? (See FYI.)

DID I MISS A MEETING?
(10 minutes)

➤ Divide into age-level small groups of three or four persons.

➤ Assign at least one case to each small group. (See FYI.) Ask each group to review the case and then to answer the questions for their age group.

Older Youth

What is going on in this scene?

Was this an occasion to see or meet God? Why, or why not?

Do you think the person(s) took that opportunity? Why, or why not?

What value do you see for yourself in meeting with God?

Younger Youth

What is going on in this scene?

What kind of changes are taking place or might take place because of what is happening?

Do you think God could be at work there? If so, how?

Do you think these scenes could be a place for the persons to see God? How?

her immediately. When he found out she was a churchgoer, he was tempted to back off; but something told him to stick with her. He was sort of shocked to find that she wanted to stay with him.

When Ray loses his temper around Andrea, her response is usually a gentle one. She encourages him to slow down and think things through, rather than just reacting. And she lets him know that she cares about him and the issue. Ray wonders why other people seem less irritating these days.

2. Serina loves learning and is an excellent student, but school is a battleground. Her father sees no great need for a female to have a good education. Most of the other students pay more attention to the stylish clothes Serina doesn't have than to what she has to offer intellectually.

Teachers usually overlook her in class except for Mr. Thompson, the science teacher. He believes Serina has the potential to become a future Nobel Prize winner, and he has told her so. He also told her he was looking into scholarships for her. Serina wonders why he is doing and saying these things for someone like her.

3. Victor and Alicia both go to the same Sunday school class. Their teacher always has lots of neat activities planned for the class to do. Sometimes, though, the teacher has them so busy doing that they don't spend time thinking. Victor and Alicia ask the teacher if the class could set aside five to ten minutes for quiet time. Some of the other students gripe that they don't want to sit and do nothing. Victor and Alicia wonder why they object.

SEEING GOD IN SCRIPTURE

From Isaiah 43:1-7
* God created us.
* God is personal, not just a force.
* God has redeemed us.
* God knows us by name; we are God's.
* God will be with us in troubled times.
* God protects us from harm.
* We are special in God's sight.
* God has special plans for us.
* God created us for God's glory.

From Psalm 139
* God knows me in depth.
* God knows my every movement.
* God knows my thoughts.
* God knows my future.
* God's protective hand is upon us.
* God's knowing is above mine.
* I cannot escape God's presence.
* God has known me before my birth.
* God is worthy of praise.
* God's works are wonderful.
* God's thoughts are valuable to us.
* God's thoughts are numerous.
* God can see if there is any wickedness in me.
* God can lead me in ways that are everlasting.

From John 14:8-24
* Jesus is God incarnate.
* Jesus' words are grounded in God's authority.
* Jesus' works are God's.
* God will enable us to do greater works than those of Jesus.
* God gives us the counselor, the Spirit.
* Commandments are from God and are important to us.
* Whoever loves Jesus will be loved by God.
* God will be made known in people who love Jesus.

HOW CAN I KNOW GOD?
(20 minutes)

➠ List on a chalkboard or on newsprint the thoughts of the group members about ways they have found to know God and be in God's presence. You may want to add your own experiences to the list after the youth have finished. Some of the classical Christian disciplines include prayer, Bible study, singing, silence, meditating on Scripture, solitude in the midst of creation, and so on.

➠ Form small groups and assign to each group an equal number of the listed ways to know God. Invite the group members to find their own space. Have an adult or older youth facilitator for each group.

➠ Ask each group to choose one (or more) of the methods on their list and to try it as an exercise in knowing God under the guidance or leadership of the facilitator.

➠ After some "practice" time, gather the groups together and ask for volunteers to share during the closing worship what they learned about God and some of their experiences with feelings, insights, and so on related to God.

GOD REVEALED IN SCRIPTURE
(10 minutes)

Older Youth

➠ Form three groups and assign to each group one of the Scripture passages: **Isaiah 43:1-7**; **Psalm 139**; **John 14:8-24**.

➠ Have the group members list on a chalkboard or on newsprint what these passages tell them about God. (See FYI, page 80.) When the groups are done, gather everyone together and have them report their discoveries.

Younger Youth

➠ Ask the participants to spread out in the room with a pencil, a piece of paper, and a Bible. Everyone in the group should read **John 14:8-24** and spend a few minutes reflecting on the verses. (See FYI.)

➠ Ask the group members to write a letter to themselves from God imagining how God has been heard and what they believe God to be saying to them. This exercise will help teens develop a sensitivity to the Spirit of God.

➠ Gather the letters and seal them in envelopes addressed to the group members. Mail the letters back to the youth sometime the following week.

WORSHIP

Create your worship space. Place symbols in the center of the circle (a Bible, a diary, a snapshot of a friend, a leaf from a tree, a musical instrument). Light a candle in the center of these symbols.

Reflect on the symbols. Each person should pick up a symbol and explain how it has been or will be important to him or her in knowing God or knowing about God.

Share stories about encountering God. Invite the participants to share their experiences of knowing God through silence, dance, music, nature, Bible study, prayer, friends, and so on.

Ask each person to also talk about some things God may have been saying to him or her, or how he or she has been comforted or affected by being in God's presence in these ways.

Close with a moment of silence. Ask the group members to think about ways they might commit to meeting with God regularly.

Sing "Spirit Song" (No. 347 in *The United Methodist Hymnal*).

Understanding Your Life Saver

by David F. White

PURPOSE:

To help youth recognize that being saved means having Christ at the center of one's life, that persons come to salvation in different ways, and that "being saved" or "not being saved" is not a Christian contest.

PREPARATION

➡ Have on hand pipe cleaners, Bibles and the appropriate commentaries, pencils, paper, and envelopes for each person.

➡ Invite three or four adults who are willing to share how they came to faith. Their experiences should represent a variety of ways of coming to faith.

➡ Gather a basket and copies of *The United Methodist Hymnal* for worship.

FOR YOUR INFORMATION

THEOLOGICAL CONSIDERATIONS

"Getting saved" implies that there is something to be saved from. There is also a sense in which we are saved for something. We as the church are called out from one state (sin or separation from God) to a new state (a right or harmonious relationship with God). The Greek word for church (*ekklesia*) literally means "gathering" or "assembly." As the gathered church, we are also called to be the scattered church, leading others to Jesus Christ and a life of discipleship (**Acts 2:42-47**).

Some people have had a vivid, transformational experience that many describe as "being saved." This conversion experience is usu-

THE LIFE-WIRE (20 minutes)

➡ Give each person two or three pipe cleaners.

➡ Ask each person to find an isolated place to reflect on his or her life with God. During the silent reflection time the participants are to make a pipe cleaner sculpture that reflects the ups and downs in their life with God. The finished sculptures might symbolize the cross, a heart, or the horizontal line on a graph that shows the individual's major movements from birth to her or his current situation in relation to God.

➡ Form small groups of up to four persons and ask for volunteers to explain their sculptures. Invite, but do not insist on, verbal responses.

➧ Then gather together and discuss these questions:

When have you felt closest to God?

What made you think or feel that you were really connected to God?

When you felt connected, did it make a difference in your relationship to your family and friends? to strangers? to nature? to yourself? Give reasons for your answers.

If you do not ever feel close to God, list some possible reasons. (This is not a judgment question!)

THE BIBLE ON "BEING SAVED" (15 minutes)

➧ Each team will prepare and present to the entire group a creative expression, such as a skit, song, rap, poem, or human frieze, to illustrate what it means to "be saved" according to their Scripture. (The Bible contains many references to "being saved." The passages we have listed are just a sampling.)

➧ Refer also to the theological information about "being saved." (See FYI, pages 82–83.)

➧ Immediately after each presentation, have the presenting group read aloud their Scripture passage.

➧ After all the performances have been given, ask:

What happened in the story that indicated someone was saved?

Is there one specific way people are saved? If there are different ways, which ones did you see or read? How would you now define "saved"?

What specific changes do these passages illustrate or call for in the life of faith? attitudes? relationships? actions? values?

Older Youth

➧ Form two teams. Ask one team to read **John 3:1-17** and the other team to read **Acts 16:25-34**. Use the commentaries to gain a better understanding of the passages.

Younger Youth

➧ Form two teams. Ask one team to read **Acts 9:1-22** and the other team to read **Luke 7:36-50**. Use the commentaries to gain a better understanding of the passages.

ally described as a very emotional, clarifying moment in which the person suddenly and powerfully understood that Christ had died, not just as a sweeping gesture for humanity, but for them as individuals. The notion that God could do something so special for "just such a one as I" is a tremendous spiritual experience.

Others have lived a more "gentle" life of faith in which their spiritual life is nurtured and grows day by day, without the dramatic conversion experience. Their faith matures through prayer and other spiritual disciplines.

Whether one's acceptance of Christ as Savior and life-center is a specific moment or a matter of day-to-day growth, salvation is not only just an event but also a way of life, based on the action of God that we accept by grace and with thanks, not by deserving.

RECONCILIATION

One of the ways in which salvation might be characterized is in terms of reconciliation. We are separated from God, from one another, from ourselves, and from creation. Salvation in Christ brings us into a journey whereby we might be reconciled to others, ourselves, God, and nature.

John Wesley taught about different "stages" in the process of reconciliation: justification and sanctification. Justification (simplistically stated) is not only God's saving action in Jesus Christ but also our realization and acceptance of the gift of salvation and eternal life.

Sanctification refers to the day-by-day presence and influence of the Holy Spirit to guide and direct our growth in faith and a life of discipleship. This continuous salvation experience recognizes that life has problems and sorrows, but that God is personally and intimately involved in our daily concerns.

The responsibility of a reconciled life of grace should include the duty of caring for others by concerning oneself with issues of justice and peace as well as telling the truth of God to others.

WORSHIP

Gather in a worship circle. Explain that it is the Holy Spirit who leads us to a deeper relationship with God. We can learn more of God in the Bible and in the traditions of the church as well as from other people's stories, but ultimately it is the Holy Spirit who draws us to God.

Offer the letters to God. Collect the letters in a basket as a sign that the participants are asking God to forgive the sinful attitudes and actions that have kept them from God, and to strengthen their faith through the power of the Holy Spirit.

Sing "Kum Ba Yah" (No. 494 in *The United Methodist Hymnal*) during the offering of letters.

Invite persons into the prayer circle. Lay on hands of blessing to those who ask for prayer.

Make prayer commitments. Pass around the basket containing the envelopes. Invite each person to take an envelope other than his or her own and to pray for that person during the week. Ask each person to mail the envelope at the end of the week.

Close with singing "Amazing Grace" (No. 378 in the *Hymnal*).

ROTATING INTERVIEWS (30 minutes)

➡ Invite three or four adults to share their stories of coming to faith with the group members. Station these adults in different rooms or in different areas of the meeting room. Ask the adults to think about theological considerations and to talk about them through their own experiences and in their own words.

➡ Direct small groups to these stations. Participants will have a brief time to ask questions of these adults about their faith journey. The youth will then move on to the next station where the next adult will share his or her faith story. This process will go more smoothly if the youth leader calls time every seven or eight minutes.

➡ After the interviews, gather the participants into the large group and discuss the following questions:

What different ways do people come to faith? Do you think any one way is better than any other way? Why?

What kinds of things led the adult guests to faith in Christ?

When some people use the word *saved* for a relationship with God, what do you think they are saved from?

What kinds of real changes were these adults able to identify that came from their deeper life of faith?

What are the things in your life that might lead you to a deeper relationship with Christ?

TO WHOM IT MAY CONCERN (10 minutes)

➡ Ask the group members to find a quiet corner where they can reflect and write a letter. Give each person an envelope, a piece of paper, and a pencil.

➡ Have each participant write a letter to God indicating what kind of relationship he or she desires to have with God. The youth might also wish to make a commitment to a different way of relating to God. The letter should also include how each person sees his or her relationship changing the ways he or she thinks about and treats other people.

➡ Ask each person to seal the letter in a self-addressed envelope. Ask the participants to hang on to their envelope for use in the worship experience.

SCHOOL ISSUES

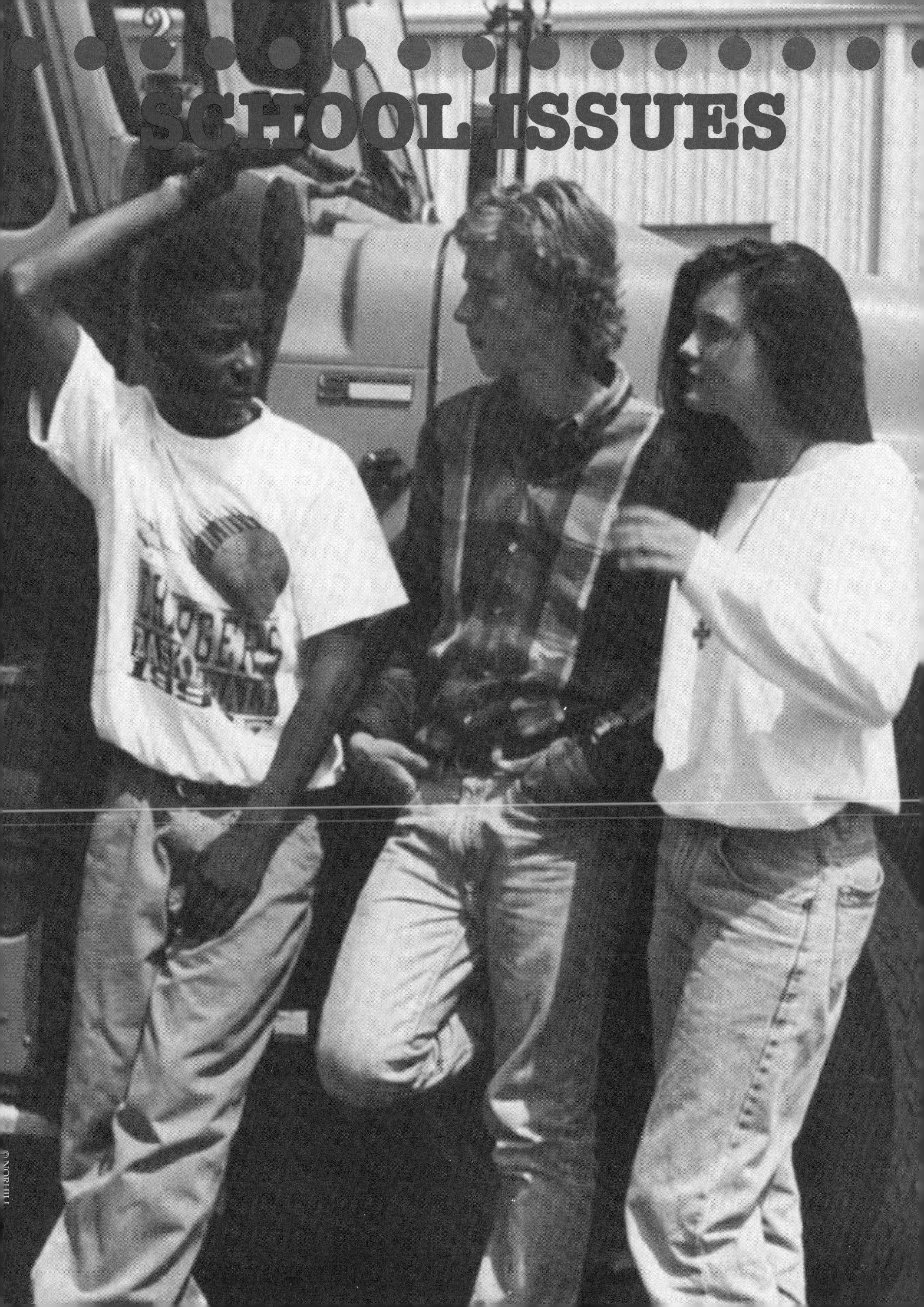

The Little World of School

by A. Okechukwu Ogbonnaya

PURPOSE:

To help youth see their school as a microcosm of the real world and to evaluate how their school experience prepares them for life in their community and beyond.

PREPARATION

➡ Gather fifty sheets (or so) of colored, letter-size paper (or a pack or two of large self-adhesive notes), scissors, crayons, pencils, butcher paper or newsprint, and masking tape.

➡ Have available newsprint and markers or chalk and a chalkboard.

➡ Supply copies of the Bible, *The United Methodist Hymnal, Songs of Zion*, and several Scripture commentaries.

➡ *Optional:* Invite a guest speaker to talk about how school prepared him or her for the "real world."

➡ Review the "Note to the Leader." (See FYI.)

FOR YOUR INFORMATION

NOTE TO THE LEADER

For some youth school is a burden, even a strange land. One reason may be the level of expectation or lack of expectation placed on that teen. For some there are responsibilities and hopes that are too high; for others they are too low. In either case, families, teachers, and other students may contribute to a learning atmosphere that is less than ideal. Be alert to group members who seem to be struggling with this program issue.

SO WHAT IS THE REAL WORLD? (5-8 minutes)

➡ Ask the participants to call out any words or short phrases that they think describe the "real world." Record these answers on newsprint or a chalkboard.

➡ Then brainstorm descriptions of life at school. Record those descriptions also. Note how the two sets of descriptions are different or alike.

THIS SCHOOL IS YOUR LIFE—FOR NOW (10 minutes)

➠ Review the background information in "School Is Part of Your Life" and the program writer's personal story of hope. (See FYI.)

➠ Post several large sheets of newsprint or butcher paper. Select three or four of the words or phrases from the brainstorming sessions that describe both the school and the "real world." Write one idea to a page. Use other sheets for three or four words or phrases that indicate differences.

➠ Give everyone a marker. Ask the participants to use the newsprint as a graffiti board to jot down the skills or information they need to cope successfully with the situations described. For example, if one similar word is "dangerous," what skills and information do group members need to cope with a school and a world that are both dangerous? If a dissimilarity is that "teachers put up with more than bosses do," what information and skills are needed for success at both school and later on a job?

➠ If you have time, mention and discuss briefly the main points of Okechukwu's story. His experience is very different from that of many US citizens who take their education for granted because it is provided free.

SCHOOL IS PART OF YOUR LIFE

School and the Community

School should not be confused with the total education of a person. It is only a part of an education that helps a person become all she or he can be within the community. There are similarities between school and the "real world," although in some cases the school is more sheltered or protected than the world beyond.

In our day, schooling is closely related to acquiring a job and the personal skills required to find and maintain oneself in a diverse marketplace. Particularly in the United States, many persons receive their first serious cross-cultural education in the classroom. This is much more true within the school than within most local churches.

My Story of Hope

School can be a place of hope and can instill a positive attitude in the face of hardship. My own story is an example. Even though I was born into a very poor family, my education has offered opportunities for a better life, not only for myself but also for future generations. Education is one way to break the cycle of oppression.

In some places in Africa children have to miss school because they can't pay the fees. Parents have to work extra hard just to provide educational opportunities for their children. Many who do finish elementary school cannot proceed to high school because they can't afford to pay the fees. This is one reason for the continuous low standard of living in some developing nations.

By attending elementary school I had gained a sense of hope, an inner awareness instilled in my heart that anything was possible.

That hope never left me. It was because of this hope that later in life I pursued an academic career. Now I have a Ph.D., which is just one result of the love of learning I found at school.

THE TOUR WALK

Prepare several tourist stations (at least four). Teams will need twelve or more sheets of the colored paper. Using the information on both the school/"real world" poster and on the graffiti poster, make small, individual posters. These smaller signs will contain words or phrases that describe school and real life, as well as coping skills and information. These signs may be made out of post-card-sized self-adhesive notes or colored, letter-sized paper.

The signs can be posted or placed on the floor far enough apart so that persons can walk between them without stepping on them. Add blank newsprint next to the posted statements so that vocations can be recorded on them.

A TOUR WALK BETWEEN LIVES (20 minutes)

➡ Prepare the tourist areas. (See FYI.) Select a volunteer tour guide for each small group of four or five persons.

➡ Identify several vocational interests. Write the job titles on separate pieces of the blank posted newsprint.

➡ The guide will lead the small group to the vocation signs. After the guide introduces the vocation, group members will help point out the listed characteristics that contribute to effectiveness in that vocation by placing the small signs or self-adhesive notes on the vocation page.

➡ Now discuss these questions:

> What information or skills did you list that seem useful for a lifetime?
> Which ones seem most beneficial for success in school? in the "real world"?
> Why, do you think, are some things helpful at school that may not help in the real world? What do you think works in the real word that is not appropriate for school?
> What are your main vocational interests now? What skills and information listed will help you become effective in those vocational interests or goals?

GUEST SPEAKER (optional; 20-30 minutes)

➡ If you have invited a guest speaker, spend time with him or her now.

➡ The guest should be able to talk about how his or her "world of school" was similar to and different from the "real world" and how school helped in his or her present vocational pursuits. Allow time for group members to ask questions. Some questions to start the conversation include these:

> In what ways are people at school different from or similar to people in the "real world"? (Remember that the world changes fast.)
> What skills do you need to get along with people at school and how does school help you develop these "people skills"?
> What skills do you need to get along with people at home, work, church, and other places? How do they compare with school skills?

STUDY THE SCRIPTURES
(10-15 minutes)

➠ Read **Matthew 5:13-16** and the commentary on this passage. Then discuss these questions:

> To what two things does Jesus compare the Christian in this passage?
> What happens when you put salt in something?
> What happens in a dark room when you bring a light into it?
> What happens to someone who has gone to school?
> How is food without salt and a room without light similar to (or different from) a person who has limited schooling?
> How can your school be seen as salt and light in your own life and in the community?

Older Youth

➠ Have teens write a letter to a friend (real or imagined) who wants to drop out of school because he or she believes that school has nothing to do with life away from school.

Younger Youth

➠ Develop a group motto or cheer that expresses how school reflects or prepares one for the future. Give the participants an opportunity to try out the cheer or reveal the motto to the whole group.

WORSHIP

Sing "He's Got the Whole World in His Hands" (page 85, *Songs of Zion*).

Say the litany responsively.
LEADER: The earth belongs to God.
ALL: Yes, the earth and everything belongs to God.
LEADER: Our lives belong to God.
ALL: Yes, our lives at school, at home, and at work belong to God.
LEADER: Our being is connected to God.
ALL: All the ways of being in the world are connected by one Holy Spirit.

Pray together. Invite each participant to offer a prayer recognizing the connection between what he or she does in school and God's purpose in his or her life.

Share future hopes. Participants may mention briefly what they hope to gain from school. After each participant's hope is mentioned, the group will say, "May God be gracious and meet your need."

Sing or say "I Want to Be Ready" (No. 722 in *The United Methodist Hymnal*). Remind the group that school is one way we can prepare for whatever God calls us to do.

Close with a benediction.

Does God Want Me to Study?

by Michael B. Walters

PURPOSE:

To help youth examine the purpose of study and their feelings about formal education. This program will help the participants separate learning for acceptance from acceptance by God.

PREPARATION

➨ Provide each person with paper and a pencil, an index card, a Bible, and a copy of *The United Methodist Hymnal*.

➨ Have on hand a calculator, newsprint, markers, and Bible commentaries for Proverbs and Matthew.

➨ Prepare for baking cookies: Get a recipe, ingredients, cookie sheets, some adult help (if necessary), and make arrangements to use the kitchen.

➨ Make the "Job Search" chart (see FYI, page 92) and collect the want ad sections from two or three newspapers.

FOR YOUR INFORMATION

"STUDY POEM"
The more you STUDY
The more you KNOW.
The more you KNOW
The more you FORGET.
The more you FORGET
The less you KNOW.
SO WHY STUDY ?

SO WHY STUDY? (5 minutes)

➨ Record on newsprint each verse of the "Study Poem" as it appears in the FYI section.

➨ Have several different members of the group read the lines of the poem in order. At the end of the poem say "Because . . ." and repeat the poem. Do this two or three times, and then ask the questions below:

> Does what you study in school relate to "real life"?
> What can an education get for you and what can it not?
> Can people study or learn for the fun of it, or does learning always have to have a goal? Give a reason for your answer.

AS THE COOKIE CRUMBLES
(45-60 minutes)

➡ Divide into two teams or some other even number of teams. Give half the teams the recipe for cookies, while the other teams must invent their own recipe. Each team must come up with at least one batch of cookies. Provide all the necessary ingredients. (See FYI.)

➡ Clean up while the cookies are baking. When they are done, pass out the cookies, making sure everyone has one from the recipe batch and one from the "invented" batch.

➡ Discuss how important knowledge, experience, innovation, and pure luck are in life. Then have the participants respond to the following questions:

> How easy was the task with proper instructions?
> How difficult was the task without written guidance?
> How did those without specific instructions go about the task?
> What did you learn from this experience?

BIBLE TO LIFE (10-15 minutes)

Have the group members research the following passages on their own or work in three teams. Provide Bibles and commentaries. Discuss the questions that follow:

✝ **Proverbs 4:1-13** (Instruction is your life.)
✝ **Proverbs 8:10-11** and **13:18** (Knowledge is priceless.)
✝ **Matthew 11:28-30** (Learn from Jesus Christ.)

> What do these verses say about learning?
> Is all knowledge as easy to get as a cookie recipe? Why, or why not?
> Is all learning "school" learning? Where else and how else do we learn?

AS THE COOKIE CRUMBLES

Place a simple cookie recipe in an envelope marked **KNOWLEDGE**. (Most chocolate chip bags have a cookie recipe. If you use this recipe, be sure to put the chips in a bowl for the second team.)

If all the teams' cookies turn out good (or bad), be prepared to talk about why and about the place information has in the process. For example, someone may refuse the information, not understand it, or have the recipe memorized and not need it (prior learning).

If you have a large group, you might want to have two representative teams work while others watch and/or advise.

Optional: Since cookie baking takes a while, you might substitute one of these activities in which one team has the answer or information and the other doesn't:

* Work two puzzles (not jigsaw puzzles) such as the wooden ones that come apart or the twisted iron "tavern" puzzles.

* Figure out brainteasers or trivia questions, giving a clue to one team but not the other.

NEWSPAPER JOB SEARCH

Cut out want ads from a newspaper that either state or imply education requirements and salary. Some ads do not state an education minimum, but one can guess from the job criteria.

Prepare a chart on newsprint similar to the following sample. ("More!" is for jobs that require more than a college degree.)

JOB SEARCH

Ad	MORE!	$$$
Ad	College	$$
Ad	High School	$

STUDY HABITS

Here are some ways to improve one's study habits:

* Break big projects into manageable chunks.
* If you hate to do it, say to yourself, *"Okay, I don't have to do this right now, but if I did I would start by . . ."* Then take the first step.
* Contract with your family for uninterrupted study time.
* Bribe yourself; for example, "When I get my research done, I will see a movie."
* If every time you start to study something comes up, get a calendar and schedule a time for study as well as play. If you plan for both, you eliminate the excuse of never getting to play. Second, plan extra activities so they don't conflict with study time.

STUDY AND VOCATION
(10 minutes)

Older Youth

➡ Put up the "Job Search" chart and pass out the want ads from the newspaper. (See FYI.)

➡ Have the group members tape the want ads on the left side of the poster, in the appropriate section.

➡ Using the salaries from the ads, figure out an average salary or a salary range for each level of education. Record the figures in the right-hand section of the poster.

➡ Discuss the following questions:

> What careers appeal to you now? Were they represented in the want ads?
> What educational requirements are requested or implied in the ads?
> Would you like a career based on the kind of job you could get with a high school diploma? with non-college training beyond high school? with a college degree? with post-college training or education?
> What other types of learning are important in getting some of these jobs? (Answers could include experience, apprenticeship, and so on.)

Younger Youth

➡ Sometimes studying better, not harder, is the key to success. Read "Study Habits" in the FYI section to the group.

➡ Form small groups of three or four persons. Have each group discuss the ideas in the FYI article along with one or two additional ideas from group members. Have the smaller groups report back to the whole group.

LOVE, GOD'S LOVE, AND ACHIEVEMENT (15 minutes)

Older Youth

➡ Have a roundtable discussion on God's love and academic achievement. Read aloud **1 Corinthians 13:2**. Some questions to begin the discussion follow:

> What does this Scripture verse say is needed along with knowledge?
>
> Does God love "A" students better than "D" or even "F" students? Give a reason for your answer.
>
> What do you think about the following statement: "God doesn't call you to be successful, but to be faithful"?

Younger Youth

➡ Put up the "opinion sheet" (see FYI). The group members will move to the area that indicates their level of agreement with the following statements. If you wish, add your own statements to the list. Discuss the participants' opinions.

* God loves me more when I get a high grade than when I get a lower grade.
* God doesn't care how I do in school.
* God loves smart people better than stupid people.
* If I pray for it, God will help me get good grades.
* A "C" that you worked very hard for is better than an "A" you got just for staying awake in class.

KNOWLEDGE TO LAST A LIFETIME (5 minutes)

➡ Have each person write on an index card one or two "God loves me . . ." statements. For example: "God loves me even when I fail" or "God loves me just as I am." Tell the participants they will use these statements in worship.

* Form a study group, and give yourselves pop quizzes.
* Select a regular study time, and stick to it.
* Ask a teacher for help with whatever is difficult for you.
* Sit in the front of the class.
* Trade tutoring: If you're good in math but poor in history, find your opposite and tutor each other.

OPINION SHEET

Use butcher paper or several smaller sheets of paper for this activity. Number the sheet (or sheets) across the top from 1 to 10. Under number 1, write "Strongly Agree"; under number 10, write "Strongly Disagree." As the statements are read aloud, have participants stand nearest the number that indicates their level of agreement with each statement.

WORSHIP

Read aloud 1 Corinthians 12:1-12.

Pray together: "Each of us has different gifts, O God. Some of us have the gift of easy learning, some have to struggle just to pass; but each of us is loved by you, and each of us you died to save. Help us to use whatever gifts for learning we have to the best of our ability, so we can be our best for you. Amen."

Sing or say "Lord, Speak to Me" (verses 3 and 5, No. 463 in *The United Methodist Hymnal*).

Have the participants read aloud their "God loves me" statements.

Pray together "Prayer for a New Heart" (No. 392 in the *Hymnal*).

Me and the New Kid

by Natalie L. Woods

PURPOSE:

To help youth deal sensitively with and welcome students who are new to their school and to provide some coping techniques for teens when they are the new kids at school.

PREPARATION

➡ Provide paper, a pencil, and a Bible for each person.
➡ Gather commentaries for the Scriptures and copies of *The United Methodist Hymnal*.
➡ Bring a ball for each small group.
➡ Provide newsprint and markers or chalk and a chalkboard.

FOR YOUR INFORMATION

BIBLICAL HOSPITALITY

Romans 12:9-13 is Paul's interpretation of the effect of love. Paul believes that it is love that creates and maintains the Christian community—love that is absolutely sincere, without a trace of hypocrisy or sentimentalism.

Love has the power to see. Divine love alone possesses the power to discern what is good and what is evil. The prime example of this is Jesus, who had no illusions about the people in his life. Jesus saw the good in Mary Magdalene, even though we question her reputation. Jesus saw the rock within Simon Peter, even though Peter had his moments of weakness and denial. Jesus saw the salvation that

EXPERIENCING UNEXPECTED CHANGES (5 minutes)

➡ Ask group members to fold their arms across their chests and to cross their legs. Then ask them to cross their arms and legs again, but in reverse order. For example, if they normally cross their legs right over left, have them reverse their position by crossing their legs left over right.

➡ Give each person a sheet of paper and a pencil. Using the hand they usually don't write with, ask the participants to both print and sign their names as legibly as they can.

➡ Now discuss the following questions:

How did these exercises feel?
If for some reason these were your only alternatives, how long do you think it would take for you to "get used to it"?
What do these exercises have in common with being the new kid? befriending the new kid? (Change is hard, but we usually find the strength to adapt and to deal with it.)

BIBLICAL HOSPITALITY
(8-10 minutes)

➡ Form groups of three and give each person a Bible.

➡ Assign each person in the group one of the following Scriptures:

✝ **Romans 12:9–13**
✝ **1 Peter 4:7–11**
✝ **Hebrews 13:1–2**

➡ Each group member should read his or her passage silently and then aloud to the group. Have the group use the commentaries for research and then decide what the common themes are in all three Scriptures. (Actually there are three: hospitality to strangers, genuine love for one another, and service to one another; but each is a call to hospitality. See "Biblical Hospitality" in the FYI section for background information.)

HELP! I'M NEW! (10-15 minutes)

➡ Once the groups have agreed upon the common themes in their Scriptures, they are to create skits using these same themes. Or, the participants may prefer to suggest possible examples of these themes instead of dramatizing them.

➡ Have the small groups choose one of the following situations to present as a skit for the entire group. After the presentations ask the actors to talk about whether they have demonstrated one of the Christian actions at school. Have those who feel comfortable doing so tell what they did and why. (See FYI.)

* I'm new, and I don't know anybody. Help!
* This school is so big; I'll never find my way around.
* I remember when I was new at my school and no one bothered to help me.
* I remember when I was new at my school and someone took time to help me get adjusted.
* Sometimes part of a school's culture is to give a hard time to the new kids or to the incoming class.
* I don't know the "rules" for how things get done at this new school, and I don't know what to ask.

might come to Zacchaeus, even though he was held in contempt by his countrymen.

Love has the power to act, enabling people to reach out and embrace others with good will.

Paul goes on to talk about love within the Christian society and the characteristics of Christians. Paul stresses that we are to rejoice in hope, to be patient in tribulation, and to be constant in prayer.

Paul believed that we (Christians) have to "walk the walk" as well as "talk the talk" about love. That means that we have to give help when help is needed and not turn our heads in an attempt to ignore a situation. We are reminded that Christianity is a corporate and an inclusive venture. We are all called to care for one another. We should expect to give and receive love from one another.

HELP! I'M NEW!

When one moves to a new school, it is a good idea to call the school's office to get the current or previous student council officers' telephone numbers. Call one or more of these persons to find out about local customs concerning new kids, any special school occasions, the bus routine, sign-ups for car-pooling, and suggested clubs or activities.

PRACTICE HOSPITALITY

Conversation Keys

* Be genuinely interested in the other person. Nobody likes talking with someone who is not paying attention or showing a sincere interest.
* Listen. To have a conversation you must hear what the other person is saying.
* Ask questions, but avoid those that can be answered with yes or no.
* Consider asking these (or similar) questions:

   Opinion: "What do you think about the new pizza place?"
   Information: "When did you move here?"
   Wild-card: "If you had a plane ticket to go anywhere you wanted to, where would you go right now?"
   Follow-up: "Why do you say that?" "What do you mean?"

Kindness Counts

Kindness. Benevolence. Consideration. Compassion. Goodheartedness. Unselfishness. Many words express that moment when a good thought translates into a good deed, when a generous gesture touches the life of another.

Though kindness is simple, it is not always easy. An act of kindness can be as simple as a smile or as dramatic as saving a life. It may cost time and convenience, but an act of kindness is done without expecting anything in return. Acts of kindness are rooted in a recognition of our own worth and the tie that binds us to God and all God's children.

HOSPITALITY PRACTICE
(10 minutes)

➡ Relational skills are learned through practice. Two of the keys to a good relationship are kindness and considerate conversation. (See FYI.)

Older Youth

➡ Have youth brainstorm ways to "kill" a conversation, such as mumbling, "Uh, I don't know" to everything, extreme inattentiveness, and so on.

➡ List the responses on newsprint where everyone can see them.

➡ Now have the youth pair up and prepare a skit based on one of the responses. For example, one person says, "Hi. Do you know where the junior lockers are?" The response each time may be, "Uh, I don't know" to whatever is asked or stated.

➡ Ask for volunteers to present their skits to the group, and then talk about the following questions:

> Why do comments or actions like the ones just presented kill conversations?
>
> What can you do to start a conversation and keep it going?
>
> What would be some needs and issues of a new kid at school and how could you be sensitive to those needs?
>
> How would you feel about acting as a host to a newcomer? How would your friends react?
>
> What biblical story can you recall that relates to being the "new person in town"? Was hospitality shown? What were the consequences, if any?

Younger Youth

➡ Form small groups of four to six persons with one ball for each group.

➡ The person whose full name has the fewest letters starts the game by holding the ball and starting a group conversation (**any** conversation) by making a comment or by asking a question.

➡ The ball is then bounced or tossed to a second person who must carry on the conversation by making a statement or by asking a question in context with the previous statement or question.

➡ This person bounces or tosses the ball to a third person until everyone in the circle has received the ball at least once. Each participant must respond within five seconds, or she or he is out of the activity.

➡ The conversation continues until there is only one person left to have the last word or until ten minutes is up, whichever comes first. Then talk about these questions:

> How did you feel when you were unable to respond to the conversation in time?
> How is talking to the new kid like this game?
> Have you ever "dropped the ball" while talking to someone? How did you handle it?
> Do you feel less pressure or more if only you and one other person (a stranger) are having a conversation? Why, or why not?

WORSHIP

Read silently "The Serenity Prayer" (No. 459 in *The United Methodist Hymnal*). Ask for volunteers to say what they think the prayer means in relation to the program just completed.

Reflect on a personal experience. Ask the group members to think about a time in their lives when something occurred that was unfair but unavoidable. Remind the participants of how they probably tried to change the circumstances, but couldn't. Ask them to remember how they felt. Remind them that they survived the situation and then ask them to think of a crisis they had some control over. Ask the group members to reflect on what they did to make things better and on the difference between the two situations.

Read "Kindness Counts" to the group. (See FYI.)

Pray "The Serenity Prayer" together.

Just What Is a Right, Anyway?

by Linda L. Pickens-Jones

▶ PURPOSE:

To help youth learn and understand some of the rights they have as students, comparing their individual rights with the rights of the community, and explore ways in which they can stand up as Christians for their own rights and those of others.

▶ PREPARATION

➠ Prepare the "rights" banners. (See FYI.)

➠ Have on hand newsprint and markers, masking tape, paper, pencils, index cards, and envelopes.

➠ Provide a Bible and a copy of *The United Methodist Hymnal* for each group member. Also have a copy of the *Book of Discipline* handy.

➠ Obtain the video "Fighting Back" *(1957–1962)*, Episode 2 from the series *Eyes on the Prize*. Preview the video and secure the needed equipment to show a portion of it. Have the tape cued to the proper place. (See FYI, "A Historical Example," page 100.)

FOR YOUR INFORMATION

"A RIGHT IS . . ." BANNERS

Make one banner or poster that says "A right is the just and fair treatment of an individual or a community." Write this phrase as a title. Immediately beneath it write "Everybody should have the right to . . ." This poster will be used as a graffiti sheet.

The United Nations Universal Declaration of Human Rights says "All human beings are born free and equal in dignity and rights." Make a second banner or poster with this quotation, including the UN source.

A RIGHT IS . . . (5-8 minutes)

➠ Post the "rights" banner and the UN Declaration banner as well as the two titled pieces of newsprint. (See FYI.)

Older Youth

➠ Provide markers for each person.

➠ Using the titled newsprint pages as graffiti sheets, the group members are to paraphrase the phrases "born free" and "equal in dignity and rights." They may jot down other ideas or images that those phrases evoke.

➠ Clarify, if necessary, the ideas and images the group members have written.

Younger Youth

➠ Point out the "rights" poster.

➠ Invite everyone to take turns completing the sentence stem on the poster.

➠ Clarify the ideas and images the participants have written.

WHAT KINDS OF RIGHTS DO I HAVE? (10 minutes)

➧ Read this statement to the group: "An announcement has been made by the school district. As of next week, only a limited number of rights will be available to the students at your school. We have been asked, as a church youth group, to decide what those rights will be."

➧ Point out the ground rules for discussion. (See FYI.) Then gather in a circle for the conversation.

➧ Use these questions to get the discussion going. Record the list of rights and limitations.

> What rights do you have as students at your school?
> What rights do you not have as students?
> In what ways do you have the right to express your feelings and ideas at school?
> Is there a group within your school that has fewer rights than others? more rights than others? If so, why do you think this is possible?
> What are the rules at your school about dress, appearance, hair styles, and so on for students? Do different rules seem to apply to the adult staff?

MY RIGHT TO CHOOSE (10-15 minutes)

➧ Review and summarize for the group the pertinent information on student and human rights. (See FYI.)

➧ Form groups of four. Each small group will select five rights that are important to the group from the "What Kinds of Rights Do I Have?" discussion.

➧ Ask a spokesperson from each small group to report their selections to the other groups.

➧ Record on newsprint the priorities each small group has identified.

➧ Have the whole group select from that list the five most important rights.

Prepare two added pieces of newsprint with "born free" as the title to one and "equal in dignity and rights" as the title to the other.

GROUND RULES FOR DISCUSSION

A ground rule for discussion is based on the First Amendment to the Constitution, which says that all persons have the right to express their opinions and ideas about what affects their lives.

MY RIGHT TO CHOOSE: STUDENT RIGHTS AND HUMAN RIGHTS

It is helpful to set the concept of student rights against the background of broader human rights.

The United Methodist Social Principles state that "We affirm all persons as equally valuable in the sight of God. We therefore work toward societies in which each person's value is recognized, maintained, and strengthened" (Par. 72, *The Book of Discipline, 1992;* page 93).

The Constitution of the United States contains ten amendments that are known as the Bill of Rights. Seven of these name specific rights and freedoms: free speech, right to bear arms, protection against unregulated housing of soldiers, protection against unreasonable search and seizure, protection against self-incrimination, trial by jury, and protection against cruel and unusual punishment.

The UN General Assembly on December 10, 1948, adopted the "Universal Declaration of Human Rights," that states, among other things, that "all human beings are born free and equal in dignity and rights" and that "everyone has the right to life, liberty and security of person."

A HISTORICAL EXAMPLE

Locate a video from the series *Eyes on the Prize,* which documents the civil rights movement in the United States. **You will need Episode 2: "Fighting Back."** Your conference media center or local library should have a copy available. This tape can be purchased by calling 800-328-PBS1 or by writing to KCET Video, 4410 Sunset Boulevard, Los Angeles, CA 90027.

Cue the tape to the portion that deals with the legal case of *Brown* v. *Little Rock School Board*, when the African American community sought to test the right of all children to attend the school of their choice. One portion is a few minutes into the tape and begins with Sheriff Mel Bailey speaking. Another is about twenty-five minutes or so into the tape and shows several of the nine African American high school students speaking.

This video is a very powerful portrayal of persons seeking the right to an equal education and helps set the issue of student rights in a broader context.

MY FAITH AND MY RIGHTS

The Scriptures can influence how we think about our rights and the rights of others. Look up these four passages:
- ✝ **Micah 6:8**
- ✝ **Matthew 5:38–39**
- ✝ **Luke 6:27–36**
- ✝ **Romans 12:21**

Some people believe that these Scriptures say that Christians should not be involved in issues that are controversial and should ignore some issues of human rights as a way of "turning the other cheek." Others believe that these

Older Youth

➡ Individually or in pairs, invite participants to write a one paragraph statement for their school newspaper stating why they believe a specific right is important. Try to have each of the five rights represented in writing.

Younger Youth

➡ Individually or in pairs, teens are to make up a poster, motto, or slogan that points out the importance of a specific right. Try to have each of the five rights represented.

A HISTORICAL EXAMPLE OF STUDENT RIGHTS (15-20 minutes)

➡ Show "Fighting Back" from the video series *Eyes on the Prize,* which documents the civil rights movement. (See FYI.)

➡ Provide a short introduction to the film. Ask the group members to be aware of their own feelings and the feelings of the people in the film, especially the children.

➡ Go around the circle of participants and ask each person to name a feeling that he or she believes was experienced by the children or other persons in the video.

➡ Go around the circle again and ask each one to name a personal feeling that watching the video evoked.

➡ Then discuss these questions:

> What are the different rights you observed people expressing or requesting in the video?
>
> What do you think the expression "the right to receive an education" means?
>
> Does this imply anything about the quality of education? If so, what?
>
> Do you agree or disagree with the statement "People take for granted the right to receive an education today"? Why?

MY FAITH AND MY RIGHTS (10 minutes)

➠ Have someone read aloud **Luke 10:27**. This is a basic biblical concept, found also in **Leviticus 19:18**; **Deuteronomy 6:5**; and **Matthew 22:37-39**. Then discuss this question:

> What does this ethical idea from the Bible tell you about your rights and those of other human beings?

➠ If time allows, explore other Scriptures that look at rights. (See FYI, "My Faith and My Rights.")

➠ Then form groups of four to six persons. Ask each group to develop a skit that portrays a struggle for student rights in their school, with an appropriate Christian response.

➠ After all the skits, look again at the list of rights developed earlier for specific school situations. Then ask:

> Have the Scriptures changed your understanding of or your feelings about these rights or the rights of others?
>
> Would you add anything to your list of students' rights as a result of examining the Scriptures? If so, what? Why?

MOVING AHEAD FROM HERE (5-8 minutes)

➠ Help the participants reflect on their own situations. Ask if there is a particular issue around which the group would like to take some action. Use these questions to stimulate the conversation:

> Do you know how your school handles the rights of students?
>
> What issues need to be explored at your school?
>
> Who are the people affected by these issues?
>
> What is the relationship to justice, kindness, and walking in God's way? (See **Micah 6:8**.)
>
> How can the group organize to address any of these issues?

passages lift up a model of nonviolent action that includes standing up for justice and human rights.

The civil rights movement in the United States in the 1950's and 1960's was based on this second idea or belief.

WORSHIP

Sing or say "Cuando El Pobre" (No. 434 in *The United Methodist Hymnal*).

Form four groups and offer a prayer of confession.
GROUP 1: "God, we are trying to figure out what is right and what is wrong; what is ours and what is another's; what we need and what we must let go.
GROUP 2: We admit that we too often seek attention for ourselves while ignoring the rights of others.
GROUP 3: We also admit we have allowed ourselves to be harmed, because we didn't remember that you created us.
GROUP 4: God, our friend, do not leave us alone. Walk with us when we go down school hallways, sit in our classrooms, and find our way to lunch. Help us to help one another as Jesus did. Amen."

Pray in silence. Ask each person to write on an index card the name of a person or group whose rights are being denied or compromised at school and for whom he or she will take a stand. Each group member should put her or his name on an envelope, place the card inside, and seal it. Put the envelopes on the worship center. Return the sealed envelopes to the writers in about a month.

Sing together "Shalom to You" (No. 666 in the *Hymnal*).

Mascots: Have I Trashed Your Name?

by Linda L. Pickens-Jones

PURPOSE:

To help youth understand the uses of mascots, the ways in which a mascot may misrepresent people by turning a group or culture into an object, and the climate of violence mascots can create in sports.

PREPARATION

➡ Provide newsprint, tape, a balloon for each person, and a variety of felt-tip markers.
➡ Gather Bibles and commentaries on Exodus and Matthew.
➡ Have a copy of *The United Methodist Hymnal* for each participant.
➡ Print out prayer 521 from *The Book of Worship* for the worship time.

FOR YOUR INFORMATION

SOME NOTES ON THE SCRIPTURE

The text from **Exodus 20:4-6** explores the idea of creating images or idols. Obviously a mascot is not an object of worship. However, such a symbol serves in many ways as an "image-maker." It creates an image of a team or a school that becomes a point of reference. It becomes an instrument around which loyalty is built. It many times creates a false image of a people, based on stereotypes or even on fears.

This use of a mascot can pull persons away from God's intentions, which are based on love, care, and respect for other persons as God's beloved creations.

GETTING THE IDEAS GOING (10-15 minutes)

➡ Put a piece of newsprint on the wall. As the participants arrive have them list every team and mascot they can think of, ranging from national teams to local school teams. Have lots of markers available for this task. Keep this paper for the worship time.

➡ Form four groups. Give a large sheet of paper and markers to each group. Ask each group to choose one of the following mascot images: Vikings, Redskins, Cavemen, Warriors, Chiefs, Bulldogs.

➡ Each small group should work together to draw an image of its mascot. Then ask the groups to list their mascot's qualities and traits on another piece of paper.

➡ Ask each group to come up with a team cheer based on the ideas they generated.

➡ Gather the groups back together and ask each one to share their drawing, their list of qualities and traits, and then to give their team cheer.

IDOLS, STEREOTYPES, AND THE BIBLE (15 minutes)

➤ Return to the small groups.

➤ Invite the group members to look at the mascots from a Christian perspective. Ask one of the participants to read aloud **Exodus 20:4-6**, part of the Ten Commandments. (See FYI, page 102.) Then discuss these questions:

> What is an idol?
> Why do you think an idol makes God so angry?
> Is God "jealous" just because God wants all the attention? Give a reason for your answer.
> How is a mascot like an idol? How is a mascot not like an idol?

➤ Point out that verse 6 promises that God will show great and everlasting love to those who love God and keep God's commandments.

➤ Next, ask someone to read aloud **Matthew 22:37-40** (the Great Commandment). Then discuss these questions:

> What is the central idea of the Great Commandment in Matthew?
> What does the idea of love have to do with the idea of mascots?

BURSTING OUR STEREOTYPES (5-10 minutes)

➤ Form age-level groups of three or four persons and give each person a large inflated balloon and a marker.

➤ Ask each group to name aloud the stereotypes that a mascot can generate. (See FYI.) Ask each person to choose one or two stereotypes and to write these on his or her balloon with a marker. Then discuss these questions:

Everyone

> Have you ever been the victim of a stereotype? How did the experience feel? How did it affect you?
> When we use these mascot images, what are we saying about our school, ourselves, and our team spirit?

STEREOTYPES

A stereotype is an image or idea about a group of people, a place, or a culture that generalizes one behavior as "normal" or "usual" for that group. Stereotypes are one cause of discrimination and contribute to other forms of sexism and racism.

FINDING THE RIGHT IMAGE

Human beings have always named actions and people as a way of identifying their characteristics. Native American people traditionally find names for individuals based on their accomplishments or the kind of person the individual is to become.

Did you know that one big university team changed its name and mascot after realizing that the name was harmful? Stanford University in northern California for many years had a famous and victorious football team called the Stanford Indians. The team is no longer called this and is now proud to be the Stanford Cardinals.

SPORTS AND VIOLENCE

Recent studies have indicated a relationship between championship football games and the increase of violence, especially violence against women. Many of the images used for team mascots are also based on violent traits or stereotypes. Exploring ways that sports activities can be times for the healthy use of the body is important for Christian youth groups. Games that build group cohesiveness, rather than being divisive, encourage the concept of nonviolent competition and nonviolent sport activities.

IDEAS INTO ACTION

Here is an opportunity to do something about the concept of mascots. Identify, as a group, a specific local or national team mascot that especially stereotypes a group of people. List some of the specific ways that the mascot creates a problem. Think of some creative suggestions for another team name. Provide writing paper for each participant to write a letter to the team or school, suggesting that the name be changed. Each letter should explain why the writer thinks it is important for this team to change its name. (Another option would be to write one letter on behalf of the whole group.)

Older Youth

Do the mascots and their qualities reflect the love ethic of Jesus? How, or how not?

How do stereotypes influence the way mascots are developed?

How important are the name and traits of a mascot in relation to the actual skill involved in playing a sport?

Younger Youth

Think of some of Jesus' recommendations for how people should act. Are these ways of living and doing found in the qualities of the mascots?

Some sports mascots are based on images of Native American people. Are these images accurate? Why, or why not?

Can a team win a game without a mascot image that is "mean and tough"? Give a reason for your answer.

➠ After the discussion ask each person to sit or jump on his or her "balloon of stereotypes" and burst it!

FINDING SOME NEW IMAGES (8-10 minutes)

➠ Form groups of two persons each. Ask the teams to think of some possible names or images that reflect pride in their own school and the important values of the school. Possible ideas: Astronauts (adventurous), Owls (wise), Cheetahs (speedy), Spiders (clever). (See FYI on page 103.) Discuss these questions:

Do these names sound funny to you? If they do, why do you think that is?

Strength is often claimed as a value, especially for sports teams. Is strength related only to violence in our culture? (See FYI, "Sports and Violence.")

PUTTING IDEAS INTO ACTION
(10 minutes)

➡ Have the group members name some ways to find out if other students or administrators are concerned about the image of their school's mascot. If there is concern, how could the youth help put those ideas into action? (See FYI, page 104.)

BODIES INTO ACTION
(10 minutes, plus play time)

➡ Develop a game for the closing that helps build a spirit of unity and cooperation in the group. Choose a game that the group already enjoys playing, such as volleyball, Ping-Pong, a relay race, or others.

➡ Ask the group to come up with ideas of how to make the game noncompetitive, inclusive for everyone, win-win rather than win-lose, and challenging. Those who prefer not to play may demonstrate or act out the qualities of one of the new mascots.

➡ Work out a few ideas and then "try them out" during the game. This new way of playing does not have to be perfect, and can be developed further another time. The idea is to take something we already do and transform it to more accurately reflect our Christian values.

WORSHIP

The hymn, the prayer, and the circle formation reflect Native American contributions to the Christian religion. These elements are chosen to counteract the violent and war-like stereotypes of Native American people that often appear in mascot images. Native peoples have contributed many diverse gifts to US culture. These three worship elements provide one means of affirming and embracing their contributions.

Sit in a circle, facing one another, with the list of mascots at one end.

Sing or say "Many and Great, O God" (No. 148 in *The United Methodist Hymnal*).

Read aloud Colossians 3:12-17.

Identify Christian traits. Provide a self-adhesive note or a piece of colored paper for each participant. Ask each person to write down one or two words that illustrate a trait or quality that Christ asks of us, such as love, hope, patience, or kindness. Then ask each participant to stick or tape his or her paper over one of the names on the list of mascots.

Pray together "A Vision of Hope" (No. 521 in *The Book of Worship*).

FUNDRAISERS

The perpetual quest for funding is something that most youth ministries face. Here, and on page 128, we suggest categories of fundraisers with some specific ideas that will help you design your own specialized events, tailored for your group and your community.

DINNERS

Everybody likes to eat. Eating out is a popular recreational and social activity, provided that the meal is reasonably priced and the service is efficient and courteous.

Suggestions for successful dinners
* Assume that the more elaborate the meal, the less profit you make. A meal that features seafood or meat will cost more to prepare than one that features pasta or subs.

* Coordinate the various facets of food preparation: meal planning, grocery shopping, cooking the actual meal, cooking prior to the dinner (if necessary). Don't forget beverages, condiments, and desserts.

* Coordinate responsibility for the "nonedibles": room preparation, permission to use the facilities, obtaining paper goods and other nonedibles, meal serving, and cleanup.

CELEBRATORY EVENTS

Celebratory functions are the perfect occasion to recognize the accomplishments of individuals or groups within the church. Your group can hire on as celebration coordinators and caterers.

Suggested celebrations
* "milestone" celebrations of church members and staff, such as wedding anniversaries, baptisms, retirements, send-offs and welcomings, graduations, getting a driver's license

* awards ceremonies for local church or community service or for local church groups, such as the Sunday school teachers or the UMW

TALENT SHOWS

Talent comes in many shapes, sizes, and sounds! Your group can organize, coordinate, and host an event that showcases these talents. Concession items can boost your profit too.

Admission charges or contributions need to fit with the type of talent you rustle up. Talent entries can come from your church, community, or a wider arena.

You can be as ambitious as your time, energy, and advance planning will allow. Invite "name" performers in addition to or instead of nonprofessional performers if you wish. Just be sure you work through the contractual and facility needs thoroughly and well enough in advance. If the cause is appropriate, some professionals may be willing to donate or reduce their fees.

Suggested talent show participants
* youth group and other members from your church or area churches

* performers from local schools; community orchestras, choirs, ballet companies, drama groups

* mimes; magicians; clowns; specialty groups, such as an accordion or bagpipe band, jug band, circus-type performers; stand-up comics or comedy troupes

GENERAL POINTERS

* Think about the event as an annual occurrence. Some things get easier in successive years.

* Be sure you have planned from beginning to end. Be aware of time, equipment, personnel, and up-front costs needed. Remember to evaluate and **write down what you did, what you need to change, and how to change it, if you already know.**

* Be sure the event is fun to plan for, to host, and to attend, even for the workers.

* Ask for freebies.

* Price tickets as reasonably as possible, while remembering the objective: to make some profit. Be realistic in your expectations.

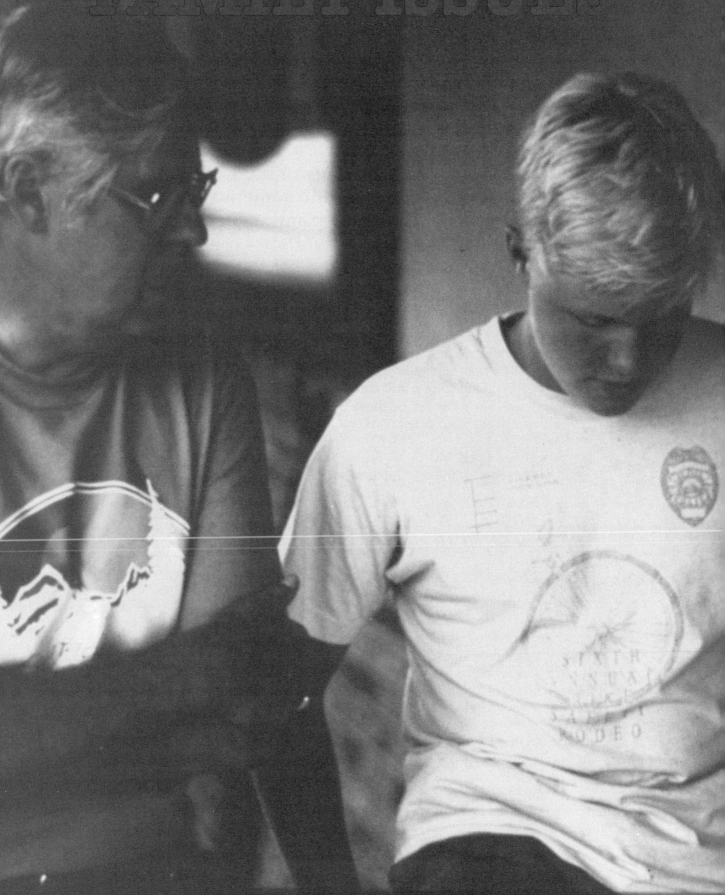

FAMILY

Does My Family Trust Me? Do I Trust Them?

by David F. White

PURPOSE:

To help youth recognize some of the ways to establish and maintain mutual trust and some ways that trust may be undermined. Teens will examine their own responsibility as well as what they expect from their family in this regard.

PREPARATION

➡ Invite a panel of three or four parents of youth and three or four other volunteers. Tell these persons they will be participating in a soda drinking contest.

➡ Bring six or eight canned drinks and three or four one-liter bottles of the same kind of soda, drinking straws, and scarves or other cloths for blindfolds. Keep the drinks out of sight until time to use them.

➡ Gather blank paper, pens, markers, magazines, glue, scissors, construction paper, and Bibles.

➡ Bring a jar of pennies.

➡ Provide items for the worship time.

FOR YOUR INFORMATION

JACOB AND ESAU

Jacob and Esau were the twin sons of Isaac and Rebecca. Esau was the first-born, while Jacob was born holding the foot of his brother. The name Jacob means "one who grasps the heel" or "one who supplants."

Jacob spent his life wrestling with other people, trying to gain some advantage from them. His brother, Esau, was the first to lose at Jacob's hands. When the time came for their old and blind father to pass on the birthright (inheritance) to the oldest child, Jacob

SODA DRINKING CONTEST (5 minutes)

➡ Enlist three parent/teen couples as volunteers in a soda drinking contest. Have them stand around a table.

➡ Open the six cans of soda on the table in front of the participants. Put a straw in each can. Blindfold the participants and have them clasp their hands behind their back.

➡ When all the blindfolds are in place, *quietly* distribute the drinks. Give each teen a can and each adult a liter bottle with a straw in it. Guide each participant to his or her straw.

➡ Invite the other group members to cheer on the teams. As the cheering gets continuously louder, silently remove the blindfolds from the youth. Invite the teens to rejoin the other group members. One by one remove the blindfolds from the parents (before anyone overdoses on the beverage).

DISCUSSION PANEL (5-10 minutes)

➠ Ask the contest participants to sit together as a panel to discuss these questions:

> How did it feel to be blindfolded?
> Why did you agree to wear the blindfold?
> What spoken or unspoken promises were made when you agreed to be a part of this game?
> How did you feel when you discovered the trick?
> How would you feel about participating in another game similar to this one?
> Have you ever felt as if some member of your family had betrayed your trust?
> Have there ever been times when you felt as if you betrayed the trust of your teen? your parent? How did you feel?
> Is it fun to trick other people? Why, or why not?
> Why do we need to be able to trust people?

For Teens Only

> What do you trust your parents to be, do, or say?
> What do they provide for you? In what ways are they consistently available for you?

SCRIPTURE STUDY (15 minutes)

Older Youth

➠ Divide into small groups of up to six persons. Have each group read **Genesis 27:1-45**, part of the story of Jacob and Esau. (See FYI.)

➠ Have each group plan a skit that updates the story of Jacob and Esau. Invite the youth to take turns performing their skits for the other teens. (You may want to assign one scene per small group instead of an entire skit.)

Younger Youth

➠ Have the teens read the narrative in **Matthew 7:7-12**.

➠ Distribute the magazines and other craft supplies. Ask the participants to make two collages, one illustrating what youth depend on their parents for, and the second one illustrating what parents depend on their children for. Display the collages on the walls of the meeting room.

conspired with Rebecca, his mother, to trick Isaac into giving it to him.

After the deed was discovered Jacob left home, fearing retaliation from Esau. Years later Jacob was himself deceived by his Uncle Laban.

Jacob continued to break the trust of others until he finally met his match. One night God came to Jacob as if to say, "I am the one with whom you must wrestle." Jacob wrestled with the messenger from God until dawn, when at last the messenger gave him the new name Israel, meaning "God rules" or "one who strives against God." This experience taught Jacob to place his faith and trust in God rather than in himself.

PEACE CHILD

In the 1960's, an American named Don Richardson was serving as a missionary in a remote, undeveloped area in the South Pacific where the native people lived in grass huts and hunted for their food. The tribes in this area had never been exposed to any elements of modern civilization.

When Richardson had lived with the people long enough to learn more about their culture, he made an unusual discovery. To the tribes in this area, treachery was a central value. It was common for these people to make friends with a member of another tribe, serving him a meal or offering gifts, only to later kill and eat him. When Richardson told the people the story of Jesus Christ, they regarded Judas as the hero.

Richardson found it terrifying to live in a world without trust. Someone who appeared to be your friend might in fact be your enemy. Treachery and death were these native peoples' main preoccupations until the day when two tribes were about to go to war.

As the missionary pleaded with the people to find another solution, he was told of a long-forgotten solution. An old tradition for both tribes involved an offering from each tribe of a small child who would live among the other tribes-people. The "peace child" became a way of establishing trust in a world where trust had long since been ruptured by mistrust. The mutual offering ensured mutual trust.

Richardson then told the tribes of a God who came in the person of a Peace Child to bring trust to the world. The missionary claimed that Jesus is able to replace fear and mistrust with peace and to show us a God who can be trusted throughout one's life. The tribe accepted the new Peace Child and the new life of faith.
(Adapted from *The Peace Child*, by Don Richardson; Regal Books, 1975. Used by permission.)

THE BUSINESS OF TRUST

In the first round, everyone follows the directions; in the second, players may break agreements. Play each round for five minutes or more.

The **banker/boss** will have a list of things for players to do that will earn them money, such as sing a song, do pushups, sweep the room, carry the youth director on one's back. The boss determines the pay for these services and can also add any number of requirements that necessitate doing business with the grocer or other "collection agents" you decide to add.

The **tax collector** will collect ten percent of everyone's income every five minutes.

The **grocer** will collect ten percent of each shopper's cash.

WHAT MAKES US TRUST?
(5 minutes)

➡ Relate the story of Don Richardson's experience in *The Peace Child*. (See FYI.)

➡ Then ask these questions:

> What are the major events in the story?
> Why did the native tribes not trust one another?
> What finally made them trust one another?
> What have our parents given us that allows our trust?
>   What do they get from us that invites their trust?
> How had mistrust become like a cycle for the natives?
> How does mistrust repeat itself for us and our parents?

THE BUSINESS OF TRUST
(15 minutes)

This simulation game will be played in two rounds. (See FYI.)

➡ Give each participant twenty pennies.

➡ Ask for volunteers to assume these roles: a banker/boss, the tax collector (who needs a watch or a clock), and the grocer.

➡ Play the first round with the banker/boss directing the activity. Play for about five minutes.

➡ Begin the second round by giving each person another twenty pennies. Announce that everything is the same except that the youth will be allowed to break agreements and established trusts. This round should last about five minutes.

➡ After the second round, discuss these questions:

> How did you feel as you were directed by the boss in round one? Did you trust the boss? Why, or why not?
> How did you feel in round two under the boss's direction? Why?
> What feelings and thoughts do you have about your interaction with the tax collector and the grocer in round one? in round two? Why?
> Did any of these transactions remind you of family interactions? If so, how?
> How important is trust in our relationships?
> What happens when trust is broken?
> Who is harmed in the long run by a breach of trust?
> Why are people tempted to break a trust?

COVENANTS OF TRUST (8 minutes)

➠ Ask the participants to scatter about in the room and to record on one side of a piece of paper some things they say or do that might cause their parents to mistrust them. On the other side of the sheet, the group members are to list the things that they mistrust about their parents.

➠ Ask the participants to write a paragraph or two about how they could work with family members to encourage and support mutual trust.

➠ Encourage the youth to show the paragraphs to their parents and to invite them to complete a similar covenant. Suggest that members of each family post the covenants someplace where everyone can see them, such as the refrigerator or the bathroom mirror.

WORSHIP

Gather symbols of home life (car keys, a cookbook, a picture of a house, photographs, and so forth) and place them on the worship table.

Sing or say "On Eagle's Wings" (No. 143 in *The United Methodist Hymnal*).

Explain the symbols. Say: "These symbols of home life relate to ways we depend on our parents and ways in which God has shown us God's trustworthiness." Pick up each symbol and talk about the arena of life it represents.

Read aloud Psalm 9:7-10. Then ask the group members to spend a few minutes considering what it means to them that they are able to trust God. Ask: "What would the world be like if God (or Christ) were not worthy of trust?"

Discuss the covenants (only volunteers need respond). Then place the signed covenants in the center of the circle with the other symbols.

Close with a prayer asking God for the strength and the wisdom to trust and to be trustworthy. Thank God for divine providence and love.

Why Can't I? Setting Rules and Boundarie.

by Michael B. Walters

PURPOSE:

To help youth explore the value of family rules and boundaries as well as their role in establishing and changing family rules.

PREPARATION

➡ Provide a Bible and a copy of *The United Methodist Hymnal* for each particpant, a "hot potato" (see FYI), newsprint and markers or a chalkboard and chalk, paper and pencils or pens.

➡ For younger youth, gather the materials needed for one of the group's favorite games. Or, provide the materials for a game of your own choosing.

FOR YOUR INFORMATION

PROGRAM NOTE

This program is about family rules and boundaries. While youth who are involved in any sort of risky or even illegal activities can benefit from the support of the youth group, more serious forms of rule breaking cannot be fully dealt with in a youth group setting. If it seems appropriate, suggest to teens who are engaging in at-risk behaviors that they consider professional counseling.

RULES—WHO NEEDS THEM!

Older Youth

Another option for this section is to have small groups dramatize one or more of the suggested scenes involving driving without any rules or guidelines.

RULES—WHO NEEDS THEM! (15 minutes)

Older Youth

➡ Have the group members imagine that aliens have secretly landed on Earth and have erased from everyone's mind any memory of rules related to driving as well as all existing records of traffic rules. (See FYI.)

➡ Have the youth imagine these scenes:
  *one's parent or parents driving to work
  *getting to school and back
  *driving to the supermarket
  *driving to a friend's house (remember that no one needs a license to drive!)
  *the parking lot at a mall

➡ Ask the participants to imagine what the situation will be like after two weeks without rules for driving. Then discuss the questions for "Older and Younger Youth."

Younger Youth

➥ Play a "no-rules game" (see FYI). Choose a [family] game that the group enjoys.

➥ Tell the youth that they are to play this particul[ar game] for a few minutes, and that afterward there will b[e a sur]prise. After about five minutes, stop the ga[me and] announce that the game no longer has any rules.

➥ Play for about five minutes more (or until th[e game] falls apart) and discuss these questions:

> Did the group follow any rules even when there [were] no "official" rules?
> What happened to the game participants? Did anyone get hurt, physically or emotionally?
> What do you think might have happened if the [no-]rules version of the game had continued for twe[nty] minutes?

Older and Younger Youth

> What good are family rules and boundaries?
> How are the rules established in your family?
> What do you think life in your family would be l[ike] without any rules or boundaries?

DIFFERENT STROKES
(10-15 minutes)

Older Youth

➥ Brainstorm various family rules that relate to such things as curfew, dating, chores, homework, and dress codes.

Younger Youth

➥ Use the "Hot Potato Brainstorm" (see FYI). Record family rules on newsprint or a chalkboard.

[handwritten note:]
Hot Potato game —
list rules on
sheet —
Ask questions on
pg 114
Read Psalms 16:
5-8
Ask questions bottom

all rule of not hurting others."

[handwritten note:]
Read 2 Tim
3: 14-17
How ought we
respond to
rules?
Prayer

responds with a family rule and then tosses the "potato" to someone else, who must either come up with an idea or say, "I pass." That person then tosses the object to someone else. The idea is to pass the item quickly, since the "potato" is hot.

Record all the rules as they are verbalized. Continue the "hot potato brainstorm" as long as it is fun and helpful.

THE COMMISSION

This activity affords an opportunity for the participants to become aware of two active listening skills: echoing and negative inquiry.

Echoing involves repeating the essence of what the other person is saying.

Negative inquiry involves using a series of questions to discover the real concern or problem.

A third skill involves looking for a solution to the problem, rather than someone to blame. The art of compromise requires practice. Consider practicing or roleplaying these skills in future sessions.

BUT EVERYBODY DOES IT!

Rules can help protect us from peer pressure. For example, if a teen is at a party and someone offers her or him a beer, he or she can reply, "No thanks. I promised that I wouldn't drink at this party, and I always keep my word."

These pairs of statements include a possible response to the initial statement:
* "I thought you were my friend"— "And I thought you were mine."
* "But everybody will be there/will be doing it/will be dressed like that"—"No, not everybody, because I won't."
* "You said you would" or "You did it before"—"I have a right to change my mind" or "I don't want to do that anymore."

Peer pressure can also be positive. Brainstorm ways the group members can help one another say yes to positive experiences, and no to options that are unwise.

The Total Group

➧ Have everyone come back together and read **Psalm 16:5-8.** Then discuss the following questions:

> Do you agree with the boundaries set by your family?
> Should all families have the same rules? Why, or why not?
> How do you feel about the process of deciding rules in your family?
> When is the claim, "Everybody else is doing it" an effective challenge to your family's rules and when is it not effective? Why?
> How else do you negotiate changes in rules and boundaries in your family?

These questions, too—

THE COMMISSION (10-15 minutes)

➧ Simulate a council on ministries meeting designed to find effective ways to negotiate changes in family rules and boundaries, especially as they affect youth. (See FYI.)

➧ Form smaller groups and have the participants discuss various options in response to the following questions:

> How should rules be made?
> Who should have the final authority? Why?
> How should one go about trying to change the rules and boundaries?
> What should happen when rules and boundaries are broken?

➧ Have each small group report its findings to the total group. Invite the participants to select one or more of the options that they think might apply to their own family situation. Encourage the group members to practice some of the options next week if opportunities arise to do so.

114

BUT EVERYBODY DOES IT!
(10-15 minutes)

➡ Form small groups. Have the participants think of some ways to resist negative peer pressure to break a family rule or to do something they don't want to do. These ideas should relate to specific situations. (See FYI.)

➡ Invite volunteers to roleplay (in the total group) one or more of the FYI situations. Encourage the other group members to react to the roleplays and to offer any additional suggestions for dealing with this kind of pressure.

➡ Discuss the following questions:

> Which suggested options or solutions might work best for you personally? Why?
>
> How would you feel if you were the one being pressured to break a rule? Why? What could you do about it?
>
> If you have given in to peer pressure in the past, what can help you resist those influences the next time? (Note that we all have a right to change our mind.)

[Handwritten margin note, left:] How can you resist peer pressure to break rule?

WORSHIP

Sing or say "Lead Me, Lord" (No. 473 in *The United Methodist Hymnal*).

Read aloud 2 Timothy 3:14-17.

Pray this prayer together: "Lord of life, we pray for those who are trying to cope with too few or too many rules; (*pause*)

for those who have a hard time talking to parents; (*pause*)

for those who are pressured by friends to do something wrong; (*pause*)

for all of these, and for ourselves, we pray. Amen."

Sing or say the first stanza of "Have Thine Own Way, Lord" (No. 382 in the *Hymnal*).

[Handwritten notes at bottom:]

2 Timothy 3: 14-17 –

But as for you, continue in what you have learned and firmly believed, knowing from whom you learned it and how from your childhood you have known the sacred writings that are able to instruct you for salvation through faith in Christ Jesus.

... everyone who belongs to God may be proficient equipped for every good work.

Siblings: Who Needs 'Em?

by A. Okechukwu Ogbonnaya

▶ PURPOSE:

To help youth think about their relationships with their siblings and discover ways in which these relationships can help them in their practice of faith.

▶ PREPARATION

➠ Secure a chalkboard and chalk or newsprint and markers.

➠ Provide three easels for large pieces of paper: one for general class use and the others for younger youth and older youth respectively.

➠ Have a Bible and a copy of *The United Methodist Hymnal* for each person and commentaries on the Scriptures.

➠ Bring a copy of *Youth! Praise* and a cassette or CD player.

FOR YOUR INFORMATION

MANU, TANNA, AND JUTA: A CASE OF SIBLING STRIFE

Manu was coming out of the counselor's office when he ran into his brother Tanna. Manu and Tanna both turned their face away from each other; neither of them said a word. The counselor, Juta, happened to notice the way they snubbed each other. Juta thought their behavior was somewhat strange, so he decided to watch the two for a while. He didn't realize they were brothers.

About a month later, Juta asked Manu who the other person was. When Manu said, "Nobody," Juta asked why he snubbed him. Manu explained, somewhat sarcastically, that Tanna "used to be" his brother

A SHORT DRAMA (5 minutes)

➠ Select three persons, two to act as quarreling neighbors, the third to act as arbiter. These volunteers should be good at improvisation. Ask them to take two minutes to brainstorm a scene and two or three minutes to present it.

SIBLINGS AS NEIGHBORS: A POSITIVE CONVERSATION (8 minutes)

➠ Have the group members brainstorm responses to the following questions. Write the responses to this set of questions on the far left side of the chalkboard or newsprint where everyone can see them.

Who is my neighbor?

Are my brothers and sisters to be counted among my neighbors?

How should a Christian treat a neighbor?

UNNEIGHBORLY AND NEIGHBORLY SIBLINGS (8-10 minutes)

➠ Play the game "I do not like it when . . ." regarding the participants' siblings. Include step and half brothers and sisters. Only children who are not part of a blended family may have other relatives who fit this exercise.

➠ Invite the group members to take turns completing the sentence, "I do not like it when . . ."

➠ Write the responses on the chalkboard or newsprint in a column marked "Unneighborly."

➠ After recording some of the negative responses, reverse the statement saying, "I like it when . . ." Write down the positive responses in the "Neighborly" column, opposite the negative answers.

WATCH FOR DANGER! BIBLE STORIES (10-15 minutes)

➠ Read aloud the case study that involves Manu, Tanna, and Juta (see FYI.) Have two or three members of the group roleplay a scene from the story.

➠ Divide into age-level groups for Scripture study. (See page 118.)

➠ After the study bring both groups together and talk over ideas for dealing with negative sibling relationships that might help avoid some of the dangers found in these Scripture passages and the case study.

and that they had not spoken for years.

Juta asked Manu if he would mind explaining why he and his brother were estranged. Manu mentioned a whole list of reasons: Tanna used to take his shoes; Tanna had dated a girl Manu liked; their parents always took Tanna's side; and Tanna humiliated him about his abilities. That last insult was the final straw and Manu vowed never to speak to his brother again. He concluded, "We have been enemies since then."

When Juta asked him if it made him happy to be so cross with his brother, Manu confessed that it didn't; but things had gone so far, he didn't know how to change them.

Juta asked if they were Christians. Manu didn't get the point right away. Then he replied, "Oh, you mean 'love your neighbor as yourself.'" But he went on to say that he had never been able to forgive Tanna and he didn't see how he ever could. And that, for Manu, was the end of the story.

A STORY OF SUPPORT: AMY AND CATHY

Amy had just returned from school and was looking for Cathy, her younger sister. Cathy always ran out to meet her if she arrived late. But today Cathy seemed to be avoiding Amy. Amy finally found her sister, but Cathy would not look at her.

Amy asked, "Cathy, what is wrong?" Cathy did not respond. Amy gently persisted; and when Cathy lifted her face, her eyes were red from hours of crying.

"Can you tell me what is wrong?" asked Amy. Cathy looked at Amy and nodded yes. Then she recounted how she had been subjected to verbal and physical abuse by one of the relatives who was living with them.

Amy knew it was hopeless to talk with the relative. This had happened before. Amy responded as she always did. "When I am older and am able to work, I will take you away. We will leave and nobody will ever mistreat us like this again."

As an adult Cathy recounts, "It was the support of my sister that helped me survive the abuse I endured as a child."

THE WESLEY BROTHERS

One of the greatest examples of the power of positive sibling relationships occurs in the context of the founding of Methodism. John and Charles Wesley were two brothers of different temperaments. John preached to the poor in the ghettos of England, while Charles supplied the words for many hymns that have been translated into various language. From the shores of England to communities in Africa, the love of these two

Older Youth

➠ Assign **Genesis 25:24-34** and provide a commentary.

➠ Do a fishbowl exercise with the biblical family in the "fishbowl." Ask for volunteers to represent Jacob, Esau, Isaac, and Rebekah.

➠ The rest of the group will observe. If your group is small, each character will observe another. If your group is large enough, assign each character to one or more observers.

➠ Each member of the family must be allowed to state what he or she sees as the problem. Observers will search out some reasons for the sibling strife found in this passage and will counsel their family member about some dangers they see in the relationship between Jacob and Esau, using events within the passage.

➠ Have the family members share their understandings of what happened in relation to the character they were assigned. Include in the discussion what the teens see as the dangers of negative sibling relationships.

Younger Youth

➠ Assign **Genesis 4:2-9** and ask for a recorder. Have the participants read and research the passage and then talk about the following questions:

What triggered the conflict between Cain and Abel?
How did Cain feel?
Did Abel know that Cain felt offended? Give a reason.
How was this strife resolved?
What does the Scripture say about the way in which one sibling resolved the issue? Do you think it was a good solution? Why, or why not?
How do you usually resolve hassles with your brother or sister?

SEE THE POSSIBILITIES: MORE STORIES (10-15 minutes)

Older Youth

⟹ Read the case study concerning Amy and Cathy. (See FYI.) You may choose to have two persons act out the story.

⟹ Assign **John 1:35-44** and provide a commentary. Then, discuss the following questions:

How would you describe the relationship between Amy and Cathy? between Peter and Andrew? Why?

Peter and Andrew were brothers and so were James and John. Do you think this made a difference to Jesus? Why? Do you think Jesus chose brothers on purpose?

What do you think the Scripture suggests about sibling relationships? about your sibling relationships?

Can your relationship with brothers or sisters be influenced by or have an influence on your spiritual growth? Give reasons for your answer.

If you have conflict with your siblings, how can you work toward healing and reconciliation?

Younger Youth

⟹ Read aloud the information about the Wesley brothers. (See FYI.)

⟹ Assign or retell the story about Moses and Aaron in **Exodus 4:10-31**. Then discuss these questions:

How were John and Charles alike? different?

How were Moses and Aaron alike? different?

What do you think God called these brothers to do? How did they help each other?

Why, do you think, did God expect Aaron to help Moses? Charles to help John?

⟹ Now ask members of the group to share any personal stories about their own positive relationships with siblings.

brothers for each other is still having an influence as their convictions, preached by one and immortalized in song by the other, continue to bless many hearts.

John and Charles Wesley helped each other in their Christian walk and shared each other's pain as well as each other's spiritual triumphs. They were sources of strength for each other.

WORSHIP

Sing together "Sanctuary" from *Youth! Praise 2*.

Read together Psalm 133.

Offer bidding prayers. Ask the group members to offer prayers related to relationships with their siblings or to other kinds of family conflict.

Read aloud 1 John 2:9-11. Have members of the group share what this passage means to them.

Pray for God's help and healing in all family relationships.

Sing "Jesu, Jesu" (No 432 in *The United Methodist Hymnal*).

FAMILY

When "Love" Hurts: Abuse in the Family

by Lynn L. Euzenas

▶ PURPOSE:

To help youth recognize the signs of abuse and neglect in the family and find ways to help themselves and others who may be in abusive or neglectful family situations.

▶ PREPARATION

➠ This program deals with a sensitive and volatile topic. Invite a trained professional to help plan the session and be present during the program. (See FYI.)

➠ Be in touch with organizations such as The Children's Defense Fund, The National Committee for Prevention of Child Abuse, or your local social service or child protection agency for speakers or handout materials.

➠ Listen carefully and sensitively to the discussion, keeping in mind that someone present may be the victim of abuse or neglect or may know of someone who is a victim. You may be sought out for help after "breaking the silence" by discussing this issue. Be prepared.

➠ Provide newsprint and markers, supplies for creating murals or posters, Bibles, and commentaries on the Scriptures.

➠ Gather copies of *The United Methodist Hymnal*, *Youth Praise! 2*, and a cassette or CD player for worship.

FOR YOUR INFORMATION

SOURCES OF PROFESSIONAL HELP

* pastor
* school counselor or nurse
* trusted teacher
* family doctor
* child abuse hotline
* sexual abuse hotline
* rape crisis center
* local law enforcement officer
* child protective service
* department of social service
* local hospital or clinic
* local youth center

WHAT IS CHILD ABUSE OR NEGLECT? (5-8 minutes)

➠ This section should be led by a team that includes a pastor, counselor, or other professional who has training and experience in dealing with issues of abuse.

➠ Form age-level groups, each with a leader.

➠ Have each group list on sheets of newsprint actions that they consider to be neglectful or abusive.

➠ Once the lists are completed, come together to compile a definition of child abuse and neglect. Talk about how the group definition compares with the definition from the Child Abuse Prevention Act. (See FYI.)

IF YOU NOTICE SIGNS OF ABUSE OR NEGLECT (10-15 minutes)

➡ Review the "Possible Signs of Abuse or Neglect." (See FYI, page 122.)

➡ Say: "If you notice any signs of abuse or neglect in a friend, inquire to see if he or she is all right and if things are okay at home. It is important to realize that the presence of any of the possible signs does not always indicate abuse, but these signs should give you cause for concern. Don't be surprised if your friend denies being mistreated, and be prepared to inquire further if the signs persist.

"Remember too that even if abused, your friend may still love and protect that family member despite the abuse, and that abusers often love their child very much. It is a confusing emotional situation to be a part of. Try to care for your friend without taking sides."

➡ Ask for several volunteers to do a roleplay. Each team of two or three persons can do the suggested scene or make up one of their own.

➡ Roleplay a family situation in which one of the children comes in late, missing a curfew. **Younger youth** will play the parents' roles; **older youth** will be the children (choose the ages).

➡ Allow the groups to decide whether normal family discipline or abusive behavior will be used. Finish the roleplay and discuss the following questions:

> How might the situation be different if the opposite type of discipline was used?
> How would you define nonabusive discipline within the family?
> How would you define abusive family discipline?
> Of the behaviors you engage in, which might be considered abusive in another's eyes? Why?

WHAT IS CHILD ABUSE OR NEGLECT?

The Child Abuse Prevention Act of 1974 defines child abuse as "the physical or mental injury, sexual abuse, negligent treatment or maltreatment of a child under the age of eighteen by a person who is responsible for the child's welfare under the circumstances which indicates the child's health or welfare is harmed or threatened thereby."

Four General Categories of Abuse
1. physical abuse: nonaccidental physical injury
2. physical neglect: failure to supply such essentials as food, water, clothing, medical attention, and shelter
3. sexual abuse: sexual exploitation of a child or youth by an adult; nonconsensual sexual activity with youth or children that violates family, social, and moral taboos
4. emotional abuse: infliction of psychological or emotional injury to a child or youth; commonly exhibited as and called verbal abuse.

Abuse or Maltreatment Versus Acceptable Family Discipline
In the nonabusive family discipline is usually an isolated incidence that is directed toward a particular action and intended as correction. The discipline is not dealt out in an arbitrary or punitive manner, nor does it have the intention of harm. After the disciplinary action, life returns to normal.

In the abusive family discipline may seem random, arbitrary, and violent, and may be used as a release for a parent's stress. Children or youth may be forced to carry out actions under threat of abusive or violent treatment if they fail to obey. Normal teasing may be stretched to the point of belittlement. Punishments may be abnormally severe and often dangerous. Inappropriate touching or sexual advances may be combined with abusive discipline or the threat of future harm should the child or youth divulge the "family secret."

POSSIBLE SIGNS OF ABUSE OR NEGLECT

* unusual bruises or injuries, or nonseasonal clothing designed to hide injuries
* fatigue, illness, hunger, unkempt appearance, and an unwillingness to return home
* depression or sudden mood changes
* drop in school performance, poor concentration, sudden skipping of school
* alcohol or drug use
* inappropriate sexual talk, provocative behavior, or unusual preoccupation with sexual topics
* nightmares, talk of suicide, or running away

IF YOU SUSPECT ABUSE OR NEGLECT

* Know the legal definition in your state.
* Understand the difference between confidentiality and keeping hurtful secrets.
* Talk to the abused person; listen carefully and take the conversation seriously.
* Let the person know that you believe his or her story and be supportive.
* Help the person understand that the abuse is not his or her fault and that professional help is available. Get help.
* If you think the person is in danger, report your concern to a professional.

IF YOU SUSPECT ABUSE OR NEGLECT (10-15 minutes)

➠ Review what to do if you suspect abuse. (See FYI.)

➠ Do a fishbowl activity in which two volunteers act out a situation and the others observe. Two volunteers will illustrate a conversation in which one suspects that a friend may be dealing with family problems or abuse. He or she will approach the friend to talk about his or her concern.

➠ Observers will discuss the approach that is illustrated and then consider these questions:

Would you handle this kind of situation any differently? If so, how?
What would you do if a friend admitted to being abused but swore you to secrecy?
Would you betray a confidence in order to get help for a friend?
What is the difference between honoring a confidence and keeping a secret?
Who would you contact for help?

WHAT DOES THE BIBLE SAY? (10-15 minutes)

➠ Ask **older youth** to read and research **Psalm 57:1-3** and **Ephesians 6:1-4**.

➠ Ask **younger youth** to read and research **Matthew 7:12** and **Matthew 9:35-36**.

➠ Have each group create a mural that illustrates the meaning of the Bible passages. After the participants explain their creations to the group, display the murals in the youth room.

WHAT YOU CAN DO AS A GROUP
(Long-term/ongoing projects)

➡ Meet with your school counselors and teachers to talk about starting a peer counseling group at your school. Many such programs, where students meet confidentially and informally to listen to other students, have been successful in getting help for students in crisis.

➡ Hold a parents' night with the youth groups. Separate the youth groups and the parents and have each group draw up a listing of what they might consider fair/unfair, appropriate/inappropriate family interactions concerning family discipline, rules, punishments, curfews, and so on.

Have each group present their list to the other, allowing time for listening and discussion. Then have both groups draw up a mutually agreed upon FAMILY BILL OF RIGHTS that can be shared with all the members of your congregation.

➡ With your pastor, work to compile a list of phone numbers of persons or agencies in your area that assist youth in crisis. Have this list printed up and distributed to all the youth and their families, and post it in the youth room.

WORSHIP

Sing "All Night, All Day" from *Youth! Praise*.

Offer silent prayer. Have the group observe a time of silent prayer, asking God to remove the negative feelings in our human relationships that can make them into abusive ones.

Make prayer petitions. Have each member of the group name one thing she or he would like God to remove so that human relationships will be free from abuse. One person might say, "God, remove hatred." Have the group respond to each petition with, "Lord, hear our prayer."

Sing or say Psalm 23 together (Nos. 136, 137, or 754 in *The United Methodist Hymnal*).

Close with "He Will Cover You" from *Youth! Praise*.

The Allowance Dilemma

by Michael B. Walters

▶ **PURPOSE:**

To help youth discover the purpose of an allowance, determine some ways to judge appropriate amounts, and explore some of the responsibilities that come with an allowance.

▶ **PREPARATION**

➡ Provide a "powerball," newsprint and markers or a chalkboard and chalk, pencils, calculators, and three index cards.

➡ Make the "Allowance Question Cards" (see FYI), number the envelopes and slips of paper, and provide a container for the slips of paper.

➡ Before the meeting assign parts for the characters in the Scripture readings.

➡ Provide a Bible and a copy of *The United Methodist Hymnal* for each person.

➡ Write out on separate poster papers "Allowance Allotments" and "Ten Commandments of Allowances" (see FYI). Gather a few personal calculators.

FOR YOUR INFORMATION

Allowances can help youth learn how to budget and be financially responsible. However, some families may not believe in allowances. Respect this idea, but encourage dialogue.

This issue can also be potentially embarrassing for some youth. Care should be taken not to allow youth to judge others based on the size of their allowance.

Older youth may face the dilemma of jobs versus allowances. For some youth, a job becomes so demanding that they have problems at home and/or at school. If this is an issue in your group, follow up with another session about jobs.

WHY ALLOW ALLOWANCES? (5 minutes)

➡ Have group members sit in a circle. Explain that there is a wide variety of experience, resources, and attitudes regarding allowances. This program will not promote parent bashing or value judging based on the size of one's allowance.

➡ Ask the following questions:

> Do you know of families who deal with allowances in a unique or unusual way? What do they do?
> How many of you get an allowance?
> Do your parents have a personal allowance?

POWERBALL BRAINSTORM ON ALLOWANCES (5-8 minutes)

➡ Form a circle and give one person the "powerball" (a soft ball or small towel tied in a knot). The person with the powerball is to answer quickly and toss the ball to someone else, who either answers or passes and then tosses the ball. Only the person with the ball may speak.

➡ Ask the participants to name some reasons for a family to use an allowance system. Record on newsprint the ideas as they are offered, and continue as long as the game is fun and helpful. Keep this record for later use.

➡ Be sure the concepts of stewardship and money management are included, but give the group members the chance to come up with these ideas first.

QUESTIONS ABOUT ALLOWANCE (10-12 minutes)

Older Youth

➡ Pass out the numbered envelopes containing the "Allowance Question Cards." (See FYI.) Draw a numbered slip from a hat or box, and have the person with the matching envelope answer the question inside. Continue until all the questions are answered.

Younger Youth

➡ Form dyads or triads. Give each dyad or triad at least one envelope with a Question Card and a pencil.

➡ Give each small group two minutes to answer each question card. Have the participants jot down each answer on the card and put it back in the envelope.

➡ Collect the envelopes, mix them up, and redistribute them. In the large group, draw slips of paper and have the persons with the corresponding envelopes share the answers with the group.

ALLOWANCE QUESTION CARDS

Write one question on each card and place the card in the corresponding numbered envelope. Feel free to make up additional questions that are especially relevant to your particular youth group. Be sure to ask for reasons for the responses.

1. When is it time to change the amount of an allowance?

2. Should an allowance be payment for work done in the home, a gift, or a set amount to cover necessary expenses?

3. If your allowance goes up, should the responsibility you have go up with it?

4. If "Jose" gets an allowance of $X.XX, shouldn't I get the same amount?

5. How does an allowance teach financial responsibility?

6. Should an allowance be used to reward certain behaviors, such as keeping your room clean or getting good grades?

7. Should everyone in the family (including parents) get a personal allowance?

8. How should the amount of an allowance be determined?

ALLOWANCE ALLOTMENTS

1. Make a list of what you think an allowance should cover in a month. Identify necessities and extras.
2. Decide how much you need to cover the necessities and how much you think is fair for the extras.
3. Consider what is fair and reasonable to request, based on your family's income.
4. Adjust your request for a rough draft of your allowance budget.
5. Make a short list of special items that you DON'T want covered by your allowance, such as an Easter outfit, or major repairs to your stuff. Place this list at the end of your budget to discuss with your parents later.

TEN COMMANDMENTS OF ALLOWANCES

1. You (shall/shall not) work for your allowance (take out the trash, clean up after a meal, and so on).
2. You shall save _____% of your allowance for extra things that you want.
3. You (shall/shall not) buy all gifts for others from your allowance.
4. You (shall/shall not) buy all clothes with only your allowance.
5. You (shall/shall not) buy all school supplies with only your allowance.
6. You (shall/shall not) buy all meals away from home (except family outings) with only your allowance.
7. Everyone in the family (shall/shall not) have an allowance, and it (shall/shall not) be the same amount.
8. Parents (shall/shall not) base allowance amounts on what others are getting, regardless of income.
9. Parents (shall/shall not) make advances (loans) on an allowance.
10. There (shall be/shall not be) restrictions on what you can use your allowance for.

STEWARDSHIP IN THE SCRIPTURES (10 minutes)

➠ Have the story characters gather together to present **Matthew 25:14-29**. Substitute allowance amounts for the different talents (and a suitable word for "slave").

➠ Discuss the allowance issues using the following or other questions:

> How did the servants use their allowance?
> Should each servant have received the same amount? Should you get the same as other youth? Why?
> Is it true that with more talents comes more responsibility? Why, or why not? What are some of the responsibilities that come with an allowance?
> What do you (or would you) invest your allowance in? Are you being a responsible steward?
> What attitudes about money and those who give it appear in the parable of the servants?

BALANCING THE BUDGET
(15 minutes)

Older Youth

➠ Post the "Allowance Allotments" list next to the list of reasons some families use an allowance system. Tell the youth to keep these two lists in mind when making a budget.

➠ Distribute paper and calculators and ask the participants to make a rough draft of their own personal allowance budget. Have them also include what they feel are the responsibilities that come with this allowance budget.

➠ Invite volunteers to share their budget plans with the group. Talk about whether these budget plans are reasonable and workable. Encourage the participants to discuss their budgets with their families and to report the results of their discussion at a later meeting.

Younger Youth

➠ Post the "Ten Commandments of Allowances."

➠ Have the group members compare the powerball brainstorm statements with the "Ten Commandments" and talk about what they think is right for them. Invite the participants also to discuss the subject of allowances with their parents.

WORSHIP

Pray this prayer together: "God, help us to grow in love and responsibility. Teach us what we need to do in our families. Help us to use our gifts wisely, regardless of the amount we have. Amen."

Sing or say stanza two of "Take My Life, and Let It Be" (No. 399 in *The United Methodist Hymnal*).

Say the litany responsively.
LEADER: All that we have is a gift from you, O God.
ALL: Take our hearts and purify them with your love
LEADER: that we may be an example of your grace in this world.
ALL: Help us to be responsible servants of your gifts
LEADER: that we may use them wisely to the honor and glory of your name.

Sing or say stanza one of "Seek Ye First" (No. 405 in the *Hymnal*).

Close with a prayer: "For Grace to Labor" (No. 409 in the *Hymnal*).

MORE FUNDRAISERS

The fundraisers that follow are for sales events. See page 106 for more ideas.

AUCTIONS

If you plan a grand-scale auction, it would be a good idea to have a professional auctioneer. The main goal of an auction is to provide items that people will not only want, but will also bid for.

Pointers for successful auctions
* **Screen donations.** If you put out a general call for donations, be clear with donators that you will screen items for quality. Refuse flea market rejects and items that do not work, are broken, or are otherwise not fit for sale.
* **Pick up and delivery.** Offer to pick up and/or deliver donated and purchased items. You may want to set some boundaries, such as size or weight restrictions. Decide in advance if you want to charge a fee and weigh that against the benefits of free service.
* **Have a "Plan B"** if rain will cause a problem.
* **Consider offering services and package deals.** Auction off services and products. A child-care package could include "free" baby-sitting, with two dish washings and a pack of diapers. A car-care package could include cleaning, waxing, and a jug of washer fluid.

SPECIALTY FAIRS OR SALES

Specialty items may help ensure the quality and desirability of the items sold. Many companies offer schools and charitable organizations products to sell as fundraisers, but you can choose your own specialties and services. Your group can plan, coordinate, and host these events, or work with the congregation.

Suggested specialty items
* **Books.** Collect, dust, and sort them. You will probably help your buyers by using specific categories: Mysteries, Westerns, Romance, Reference, Self-help, and so on. Some collectable magazines can augment the offerings too.

* **Art, crafts, and toys.** These items can be donated or purchased at a discount from local vendors for resale, or sold directly by the vendor who has purchased a sales space at the fair. You can make and sell your own items, priced competitively.
* **Clothing.** Offer "customized" clothing, such as personalized T-shirts, decorated sweat shirts, handworked leather belts and purses, seasonal or novelty items (such as Christmas socks), handmade and decorated neckties, and jewelry.
* **Personalized services.** These could include beauty makeovers, pet grooming, preparation of "gourmet" meals or snacks, shopping services, or housekeeping services.

"THONS" AND SPORTS EVENTS

Pledge-per-unit money raisers require the participation of the few and allow the donors to stay home. You'll need pledge sheets and a clear means of collecting the pledges so that they are clearly charitable donations. Benefit sports events need the participation of spectators/donors and have a greater "fellowship factor" than "thons." Concession sales will boost your profits.

Suggested "thons" and sporting events
* **Walk, run, bike, hike, rock, dance, swim, or otherwise move** from here to there with a pledge per mile, kilometer, hour, lap, or whatever. (Some teens might excel at a sleep-a-thon or phone conversation-a-thon!)
* **Active sports events.** Get together church or neighborhood intergenerational teams or youth groups for some friendly competition. Be sure that you have the use of the playing area.
* **Passive games or competition** are good intergenerational mixers. Checkers, chess, cards (no gambling), or other popular board games may be the ticket for persons who are not into active sports. Players pay to play for a designated time or for each point scored or game won.

PUBLIC ISSUES

Gang Life: A Christian Perspective

by Linda L. Pickens-Jones

PURPOSE:

To help youth understand some of the reasons teenagers join gangs and assess the potential worth or appeal of gang membership. This program distinguishes between gangs, clubs, and teams.

PREPARATION

➠ Prepare colored ribbons (see FYI) and give one to each person as he or she arrives.

➠ With two or three teens, monitor the print and electronic media news reports for two weeks before the session. Cut out or record any references to gangs. Write short excerpts on newsprint and post them prior to the session.

➠ Prepare the "Gang Youth Identity" cards. (See FYI.)

➠ Provide a Bible and a copy of *The United Methodist Hymnal* for each member.

➠ Gather paper, pencils, tape, index cards, newsprint, and markers.

FOR YOUR INFORMATION

TIE A RIBBON

From two different colored spools of ribbon, cut an equal number of lengths. Each person is to tape the ribbon to his or her wrist or clothing. Arrange for two **older youth** to receive a third color ribbon.

DO YOU WANT TO JOIN?

The "Gang Youth Identity" cards provide some fictional case studies that will help the participants understand gangs. From a Christian standpoint a gang member is a unique and special person in the eyes of God. Any learning about gangs needs to affirm the humanity

INTRODUCTION (5-8 minutes)

➠ Review the general information on gangs (see pages 132–133) and introduce the program. Ask each participant to write down three words or ideas about gangs that he or she has heard, believes, or has experienced.

➠ List the ideas on newsprint so everyone can see all the different ideas about gangs. Talk about them briefly.

DO YOU WANT TO JOIN?—A ROLEPLAY (10-15 minutes)

➠ Form two "gangs" identified by their ribbons. Each gang is to choose an identifying name and develop a handshake or other group signal. The third group will not be a gang and will have no group name or symbol. Then reassemble so each group can tell its name and show its sign. (See FYI.)

➠ Hand out the "Gang Youth Identity" cards. The two cards designated for **older youth** feature teens who are struggling with gang membership. Give the participants time to flesh out their identities. (See FYI, "Gang Youth Identities.")

⇒ Ask each member to introduce himself or herself by saying: "I am *(gang member name)* and I am part of the *(gang name)*." The persons who are not part of a gang will also introduce themselves and talk briefly about what it's like to be separate from the other two groups.

WHAT DO THE MEDIA SAY? (10-15 minutes)

⇒ Review the posted media statements and the class ideas about gangs. Discuss the following questions:

> Now that you have "met" some gang members, do you see the description of gangs and gang members any differently? Why, or why not?
> What would you change about the list?

Older Youth

> Ideas about gangs are often negative. Are there any positive reasons for being a part of a gang? If so, how do these relate to the negative reasons?
> What do you think is the reason people become part of a group that becomes violent? Are all people in gangs violent?
> If you are not in a gang, and you started a friendship with someone who was identified with a gang, what would you say to the person who wants you to join the gang?
> Jesus said that we are to "love our enemies." What does that mean in the context of gang membership?

Younger Youth

> Why do people join gangs?
> What groups do you belong to? How are these the same as gangs? How are these different from gangs?
> What would you say to a friend who wanted you to join his or her gang?

of gang members, acknowledging the complex human situation in which these youth find themselves. The case studies are designed to illustrate what leads people to do the things they do, rather than any particular lifestyle. More than one person can share an identity or you can add others.

Note: Remind the group members that each person is "acting," not talking about himself or herself.

GANG YOUTH IDENTITIES

Photocopy each case study (there are more on page 132) and affix it to an index card.

* James is thirteen. His brother was not a gang member but was killed in a drive-by shooting. James decided the best protection was to join a gang.

* Michael is seventeen and has already served time for burglary. He doesn't know his father, and his mother puts in long hours as a housekeeper. He's been working with several other "gang bangers" to set up a gang truce.

* Joanna is fifteen and is expecting a baby. She dropped out of school because her mother told her she was stupid. Joanna says she will love her baby more than her mother loves her. Joanna wants to become a doctor.

* Lily just moved into the neighborhood. Her parents are old-fashioned, and speak only Mandarin Chinese. They are always telling her to be careful. Lily secretly had her ears pierced to be like a group of new friends.

* Solana is tired of her father and brothers harassing her. She has become tight with Baldo, somebody she trusts to know about her troubles. Everyone says he's mean, but he watches out for her. Solana wonders what to do.

* Carlos escaped across the border into the US when he was twelve. Both of his parents were killed in the war in El Salvador. He hasn't learned much English, so he doesn't understand a lot of what goes on at school. The school officials say he is just a trouble maker.

* Linh is from Vietnam. He grew up in a refugee camp. The only way to survive there was to fight and sell drugs. He doesn't see that the US will be any different.

* Marta is thirteen and recently took her first Holy Communion. Her parents are devout Roman Catholics. Church is important and safe for Marta, but she wonders what the church has to do with the things that happen every day at school.

* "Speed" is a school dropout. He is embarrassed to be six feet tall and still unable to read. He hangs on the street corner near the school and wonders what it would be like to own his own business. His beeper goes off and he takes care of another drug run.

For Older Youth

* Roxanna loves school, but doesn't have many friends. She lives with her grandmother and has a job after school doing grocery shopping for several "shut-in" neighbors.

* Jerry is new to the community and really misses his old friends. They used to mess around, breaking into places to take a few things; but it sure wasn't a "gang" like the ones in his new neighborhood.

THE GANG AT THE VINEYARD (10 minutes)

➡ Ask the participants to read **Mark 12:1-9**. Jesus does not portray the tenants as gang members, and his purpose is prophetic. The tenants do join forces for their own benefit, which is one characteristic of gangs. Taking the events at face value, talk about these questions:

> What are the values expressed by the tenants? Are any of them similar to those of a gang? How?
> What did they hope to accomplish? Did they succeed?
> The violence of the tenants led to violence by the owner. How is this like gang activity?
> How might you rewrite the end of this story to bring it in line with Christian values?

AN INTRODU

"Drive-by shootings." "Gang-bangers." "Gang apparel." These terms and others fill the media. But what do they mean? What are gangs and who is in them? Gangs aren't something new. They have been part of the US for several centuries. Gangs often are established in the midst of poverty and despair. Other gangs organize in wealthy communities. While we hear about violence in gangs, they can be a place for security and belonging for the people who are in them. How do Christians understand gangs? What does our faith teach us about this subject?

In many cities the issue of gang violence has become the focus of political action. Political leaders are elected because they promise more police protection. Other community leaders believe that ending gang violence is connected with ending other social violence and with strengthening the economy.

In Los Angeles, California, a coalition of gang leaders of the Bloods and the Crips have negotiated a truce. They decided that it was time to stop killing one another, and that they all had the same struggles. This truce has ended decades of old prohibitions against crossing over into another gang's territory, even to go to the grocery store.

One gang member said, "I have to believe there will be change. I just need a job. I have five brothers, and I don't want it to be the same for them. I have never been anywhere but this project and the jail. All I've ever seen is

WHERE DO WE GO FROM HERE?
(10-15 minutes)

⇒ We can make a difference! Gang members often say they would stop being "gang bangers" if they had jobs, if schools provided a decent education, and if childcare was available for teenage mothers. Discuss these questions:

> What do you think of these ideas?
> What could your church do for youth in gangs?
> What might your newly met "gang member friends" say and want?
> What programs already exist in your community?
> What could you say to someone you know who is a member of a gang?

N TO GANGS

what I see out of the window of the police van as they take me to jail. I just need a job for some money."

Another group of gang members, through a church sponsored program called *Proyecto Pastoral*, are working steady jobs and some are going to school as well, making "Homeboy Tortillas" and "Homeboy Bread."

One community group called *Common Ground Foundation*, directed by Mr. Fred Williams, seeks to "reclaim" youth from the street. Based at a Los Angeles junior high school, former school dropouts and "gang bangers" walk the streets, finding youth who are hanging out and talking with them about their problems. It usually takes at least twenty-five hours of direct intervention for these youth to agree to return to school.

Young women in gangs often become mothers while they are still teenagers. They speak of the hope of providing a more loving atmosphere for their baby than they have experienced. For some young women the baby is the only thing they believe is really "theirs." Children bring status to young women in gangs. Often, however, they do not have the monetary or emotional support necessary to raise the children in the way they have dreamed.

(This information was obtained from conversations with participants in *Proyecto Pastoral*, Dolores Mission, East Los Angeles; *Common Ground Foundation* in South Central Los Angeles; gang members in Los Angeles; and newspaper reports.)

WORSHIP

Gather and sit in a circle.
Read 1 Corinthians 12:12-17 as a litany. Divide the Scripture so that the "gang groups" each take turns reading a portion in unison.

Ask each person to remove her or his ribbon and tie it to the ribbon of the next person. When the tying is finished there will be a large circle of ribbon. Place the ribbon circle on the floor in front of the group.

Pray together this prayer: "God of all people, we ask for your presence with each one of us. When we are lonely, help us know we have friends who can help. When we meet other lonely people, help us to provide friendship and hope.

"We pray for gang members and for their families. We pray for those who have been hurt by gangs, both as members and as victims. We ask you to guide us as we find a way to end all kinds of violence in our society. We pray in the name of Jesus. Amen."

Sing or say "Help Us Accept Each Other" (No. 560 in *The United Methodist Hymnal*).

RESOURCES FOR FURTHER STUDY

"Gangs With a Vision of Peace," *Christian Social Action*, June 1993, pages 14–16. A publication of the General Board of Church and Society of The United Methodist Church.

Gangs, by Karen Osman (Lucent Books, 1992). A book in the Lucent Overview Series.

Sojourners Magazine, August 1993. Special issue on the gang truce.

"*Dreams on Fire*." A film about gangs, produced by Franciscan Films.

Who's Homeless?
Who's Hungry?
Who Cares?

by A. Okechukwu Ogbonnaya

CROP

PURPOSE:

To introduce youth to the plight of poor and homeless people in a way that leads teenagers to think socially and theologically about their personal response and their sense of Christian obligation to care for others.

PREPARATION

➥ Invite a staff member (and a resident or guest, if possible) from a local shelter to make a presentation. Ask the speaker to be prepared to discuss the working philosophy of the shelter and to provide a copy of this philosophy in writing if it is available. (See FYI.)

➥ Find statistics related to hunger and homelessness in your immediate area, the US, and the world. Review the HPI and Society of St. Andrew information. (See FYI.)

➥ Provide a Bible for each person and commentaries on the Scripture passages.

➥ Bring the supplies for the worship service.

FOR YOUR INFORMATION

OPTION: VISIT A SHELTER

Do this program first as preparation for visiting a shelter or extend the program to include the visit, so that group members have a hands-on experience. Secure permission from the managers of the shelter to visit and from parents of youth who will be involved. Extend an open invitation to parents who want to participate.

GATHERING AND CENTERING
(8-10 minutes)

➥ Invite volunteers who have helped feed the hungry or who have helped provide shelter for the homeless to briefly comment on the way they felt the first time they got involved in an experience of this kind.

➥ Ask those who have not participated yet to talk about their fears and their presumptions concerning persons who are homeless or hungry. This participation could take the form of sentence prayers.

WHERE IS HOME FOR THE HOMELESS? (20-30 minutes)

➥ Invite the guest speaker from the shelter to talk about a "routine" day and about the philosophy that undergirds the ministry of the shelter. Leave some time for questions.

➥ Part of the conversation should include dealing with issues and misconceptions about homelessness and hunger. Suggested comments and questions include these:

* Who are the clients of the shelter? How are they alike? How are they different?
* Does your shelter serve teenagers? If so, what are the reasons for their need? If not, what do homeless teens do?
* What services does the shelter offer? What is not offered?
* What are a "typical" day and evening like (if there is such a thing)?
* What are the most pressing health and safety issues?
* How do you deal with the myth that there is not enough food available to feed everyone?
* What can be done about this attitude: "I don't have to get involved; there are institutions to do the work"?
* How can we counteract the notion that homeless and hungry people are just lazy?

➥ If you plan a visit to a shelter, ask the staff if the group members can do any of the following activities or others that the staff identifies:

* Help with one of the meals.
* Help register clients for shelter for one night.
* Share in the meal.
* Talk with a client of the shelter.

WHAT I CAN DO: KNOW THE FACTS

* Hunger affects over 1.3 billion people in the world.
* Over 25 million people suffer from hunger in the United States.
* Over 12 million children die every year from hunger-related illnesses (approximately 35,000 a day).
* Every fifth child in the United States lives below the poverty line and faces hunger.

(From *Hunger 1994: Transforming the Politics of Hunger*, a study conducted by Bread for the World Institute.)

THE HEIFER PROJECT INTERNATIONAL (HPI)

The United Methodist Church participates in the Heifer Project program to feed the hungry by providing livestock that can provide long-term food. The Heifer Project donates animals and teaches local communities how to raise them.

Your youth group may want to contact the Heifer Project office near you for information on how to participate:

* **Headquarters**: HPI, P.O. Box 808, Little Rock, Arkansas 72203; phone 800-422-0474
* **Mid-Atlantic**: HPI, P.O. Box 188, New Windsor, Maryland 21776
* **Northeast**: HPI, 216 Wachsett Street, Rutland, Maine 01543
* **Southeast**: HPI, P.O. Box 2185, Sanford, Florida 32772
* **Great Lakes**: HPI, P.O. Box 767, Goshen, Indiana 46526
* **Great Plains**: HPI, P.O. Box 4527, Topeka, Kansas 66604
* **Southwest**: HPI, P.O. Box 1968, Whittier, California, 90609
* **Northwest**: HPI, P.O. Box 126, Ceres, California, 95307

THE SOCIETY OF ST. ANDREW

The United Methodist Church is in covenant with the Society of St. Andrew to minister to hungry people within the United States.

Through the Society's Potato Project Christians committed to heal the problem of hunger can respond by learning about hunger, raising funds to support the Society's programs, and participating in one of the gleaning programs.

For more information write to The Society of St. Andrew, P.O. Box 329, State Route 615, Big Island, VA 24526. Or call 800-333-4597.

WHAT CAN I DO? "GIVE US THIS DAY OUR DAILY BREAD"

This particular phrase in the Lord's Prayer follows two crucial phrases: "Thy Kingdom come," and "Thy will be done on earth as it is in heaven."

The placement of the third phrase is crucial since there can be no genuinely divine kingdom where one person is still hungry. The will of God cannot be fully realized as long as the bare necessities of life elude some people.

The Kingdom and the will of God are made concrete in the bread. The nourishment of the body, which is the temple of God, is vital to the continuous spreading of the gospel and the transformation of life. There can be no Kingdom without bread.

Finally, note that the prayer does not say "give me." The plurals indicate our responsibility for others. The wording underscores our connection with the hungry of the world who are themselves children of God. The bread that I eat is our bread, not my bread alone.

CARING FOR "THE LEAST" (15 minutes)

Older Youth

➡ Assign **Matthew 25:31-46** and provide commentaries. Ask the group members to read and research the passage and then to discuss these questions:

> What is the difference between the sheep and the goats?
> What are the characteristics of the sheep? of the goats?
> Who is the Son of Man?
> What are the rules for deciding how to separate the sheep from the goats?
> What does that mean for us?
> How can we become more "sheeplike"?

Younger Youth

➡ Assign **Deuteronomy 24:10-13, 19-22** and provide a commentary. Ask the group to read and study this passage and to answer these questions:

> What did God ask the people to do? Why?
> For whose benefit were these commands given?
> How would you apply these rules today?

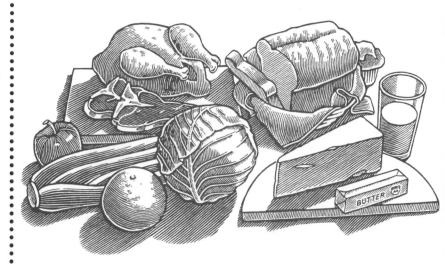

BUT WHAT CAN I DO? (15 minutes)

➥ Review the statistics on poverty and hunger. (See FYI, page 135.) Have the group members summarize their own experiences so far.

➥ Discuss what all this means in terms of the group members' commitment to the gospel of Jesus Christ. Remind the participants of the words of the Lord's Prayer, "Give us this day our daily bread." Reflect on the personal and practical implications of this request. (See FYI, page 136.)

➥ Have the participants imagine an ideal world. Ask for quick, brief responses to these questions: What would you do about hunger if you were in charge? What would you do about homelessness if you were in charge?

➥ Brainstorm for short-term or long-range projects your group can do to address local issues of hunger and homelessness, such as starting or participating in a local soup kitchen or shelter, or other hunger/homeless projects like the gleaning program of the Society of St. Andrew and Heifer Project International. (See FYI, page 135.)

➥ If you can begin planning now, address these questions:

What are the needs of our community?
Who is trying to meet those needs? Can we join forces and be more effective, or should we operate on our own?
What kind of budget do we need? How can we raise the money?
Who is available to help?
What kind of special training or orientation do we need? How can we get it?
How can we include children or middle school/junior high persons as well as older youth and adults?

THE CLOSING ACT (5 minutes)

➥ Invite the group members to talk about this program and how the Scriptures relate (or do not relate) to their experience.

WORSHIP

Gather around a large table. In the center of the table place a basket of Hawaiian rolls, a basket of fruit, and a beverage with cups.

Sing "We Are One In the Spirit" (No. 975 in the *Supplement to the Book of Hymns*).

Offer sentence prayers. Have the participants pray for a compassionate attitude toward persons who are hungry or homeless and for the persons themselves.

Celebrate the worship meal. Invite the members of the group to take turns selecting a dinner roll, a piece of fruit, and a beverage from the center of the table and then return to their place. Each person is to offer the food and drink to the participant on his or her right.
The giver will say, "May the kingdom of God come; may God's will be done on earth as it is in heaven."
The receiver responds with, "May God give us this day our bread to eat."

Read aloud James 2:14-17.

Close with the Lord's Prayer.

TO DO MORE
See the related mission projects in the *UMY Mission and Event Annual:* "Lend Two Hands to Fight Hunger," pages 60–63 and "Homelessness in the United States," pages 76–79.

Is the US Number One?

by Linda Pickens-Jones

PURPOSE:

To enable youth to know that they can be proud of their personal heritage and their national identity without feeling better than or superior to other nations or cultures.

PREPARATION

➡ Print the "Opinion Poll" (see FYI) and the selection committee statement (see page 140) on newsprint or a chalkboard before the program begins.

➡ Record the information regarding each role on an index card (see page 139).

➡ Provide paper and pencils, a Bible, and a copy of *The United Methodist Hymnal* for each participant. Bring a commentary on Isaiah.

➡ Gather paper and paints or drawing markers for the mural.

➡ Find a globe and flags for the worship center.

➡ Arrange for someone to sing the hymn "This Is My Song."

FOR YOUR INFORMATION

OPINION POLL

1. Citizens of a country should always stand by their country, right or wrong.

2. If you criticize the United States, you are hurting this country.

3. I don't think there should be such a thing as national boundaries. Everyone should be a "citizen of the world."

4. I believe it is patriotic to criticize the things the government of the United States is doing.

5. The United States of America is the only free country in the world.

6. There are many different countries that work for freedom.

7. I don't think I should have to learn about other cultures when my culture is what I like best.

WHAT IS YOUR OPINION?
(8-10 minutes)

➡ Say: "There is nothing wrong with being proud of one's country and one's heritage. In fact, it is important to honor who we are and our place of origin. So what's the issue here? The fact that we're all from different places and different backgrounds, means that we have different ideas. Is the US number one and what does that mean, anyway?"

➡ Take an opinion poll using the printed statements (to which there are no right or wrong answers). (See FYI.)

➡ Write the opinion options where they can be seen: "agree completely," "agree somewhat," "unsure," "disagree somewhat," or "disagree completely."

➡ Have the group members number a piece of paper from 1 to 10. Then read each statement aloud, giving time for each person to record one of the above responses.

➡ After everyone has answered the questions, take a poll to see what the participants believe about God and country. Spend some time discussing the answers.

EXCHANGING PLACES: A ROLEPLAY (15-20 minutes)

➡ The focus of the roleplay is to explore how a student might handle the thought of going to another country as an exchange student. The purpose of the roleplay is to help each participant explore the idea of patriotism and what impact it has on one's relationship with people from other countries. (See FYI.)

➡ One of the exchange students will be going from the US to Japan, and the other exchange student will be coming from Russia to the US.

➡ Form two small groups. Have each group work on the same roleplay. The roles can be expanded or reduced as needed for your group size. Hand out the index cards that contain the following role descriptions:

* **Chairperson**—You make sure that everyone has a chance to speak and remind people to listen to one another.

* **Exchange student**—You have conflicting feelings about living in another country for a whole year, because your country, as far as you are concerned, is number one.

* **Friends**—You will represent a variety of opinions.

* **Teacher**—Your role is to do some explaining of ideas like "patriotism," "nationalism," and "what it means to be a US citizen." (See FYI.)

* **Parent (or parents)**—You ask a lot of questions to make sure your son/daughter will be safe.

* **Selection committee**—You need to know whether the student is going to be flexible and accepting of another culture.

* **Pastor**—You will help remind people of Christian beliefs. Be aware of the stance of The United Methodist Church. (See FYI.)

* **A representative from the "host" country**—You want the exchange student to be accepting of your country and customs.

8. I like learning about other cultures because it helps me to be a more well-rounded person.

9. God has a special role for the US to play in the world.

10. Christians have a special role to play in bringing unity in the world.

EXCHANGING PLACES GUIDELINES

For the Roleplay:

1. Remember that this is a roleplay and not the real thing.

2. Listen to the person speaking, and then make your point.

3. Try to think about things from the point of view of the person you are representing.

4. Leaders: Help the discussion be active yet respectful. Some stereotyping may arise during the roleplay. Help to correct these stereotypes whenever possible.

Helpful Terms

Nationalism refers to devotion to one's nation, and *patriotism* adds the dimension of fervency or zeal.

Who Is an American?

Many people who live in the United States use the term *American* to refer to their own country. But *American* can refer to all the nations of both North and South America. A person in Brazil or El Salvador is just as much an *American* as a person from Colorado or New York or Georgia!

What Is a Nation?

People have different understandings of the word *nationhood*. Did you know that there are other nations within the boundaries of the United States? The native peoples of the Americas have their own sovereign nations, and thus there exists the Navajo Nation, the Cherokee Nation, and the Iroquois Nation, among others.

THE UMC STANCE

The 1992 *Discipline* states that "God's world is one world. . . . We commit ourselves, as a Church, to the achievement of a world community that is a fellowship of persons who honestly love one another. We pledge ourselves to seek the meaning of the gospel in all issues that divide people and threaten the growth of world community . . . . As individuals are affirmed by God in their diversity, so are nations and cultures." (From Paragraph 75, "The World Community," pages 104–105.)

➡ Instruct the selection committee to read aloud the following statement:

* Congratulations. You have been selected to be an exchange student for the International Christian Youth Exchange. You will be spending one year in (group 1 in Japan; group 2 in the US). We have called you, your family, and some friends here today to clarify your suitability for this exchange program.

➡ Ask the exchange student to make a statement about why she or he wants to be an exchange student. Then everyone can join in a lively discussion!

➡ Debrief afterward. This time of discussion is really important. Lots of feelings may have surfaced during the roleplay. Have the groups come back together. Ask each group to share what happened in their group. Then, open the discussion for everyone.

How did you feel during the discussion about the idea that "The US Is Number One"?
What did it feel like to play the position you were asked to take?
Do you have a different understanding of nationalism or patriotism than you did at the beginning of the session? If so, how has your understanding changed?

GOD OF ALL THE NATIONS
(15 minutes)

➡ Assign **Isaiah 49:1-6**. Have the participants read and research the passage.

➡ Take a look at the hymn "This Is My Song" (No. 437 in *The United Methodist Hymnal*). Invite a choir member or someone who is comfortable singing in a group. Ask her or him to sing the song, and then lead the group in singing it. (Or read the stanzas aloud.)

➡ Talk about the Scripture and the song with one another using the following questions:

> What does the idea of "God of all the nations" mean to you?
>
> Do you think we can hope and pray for peace in other countries, and even help accomplish it politically, without feeling as if our own country is number one? Give reasons.
>
> What does this song say about other people's hopes and dreams?
>
> What feelings are expressed about one's own land?
>
> What are some of your hopes and dreams?
>
> What is your favorite part of your land?
>
> What would a "song of peace" be like?
>
> What do you think it means to be a light to the nations?

➡ Provide a large sheet of paper and paints for the group. Ask the participants to draw a mural that expresses the ideas in "This Is My Song."

➡ Plan to share the mural with the congregation in the next several weeks. Also check with the worship leaders about singing "This Is My Song" during the church's worship service.

WORSHIP

Create a worship focus with a current globe or world map and different national flags on a table.

Read and reflect on the Scripture. Assign each of four small groups a different Scripture:
✞ **Deuteronomy 10:17-19**
✞ **Mark 10:42-45**
✞ **Acts 10:34-35.**
✞ **Romans 12:9-10**

Ask the group members to read and discuss their text. Then each group should use the ideas in the Scripture to complete this sentence: "Some people say that America is Number One. As Christian youth we say . . ."

Each group will read aloud its statement.

Pray for our nation. A beautiful prayer for the nation was written by Toyohiko Kagawa, a famous twentieth-century Japanese Christian, who was aware of how nationalism can cause suffering. He wrote this in Japan, after World War II. Read together "For Our Country" (No. 429 in *The United Methodist Hymnal*).

Pray for all nations. Ask six participants to go to the globe and to each select the name of a country, at random. After a short silence, each person who has selected a country will take turns calling out the country's name. After each nation is named, the group responds:

"We pray for all the people of this nation, with love, O God."

Read or sing together stanza three of "This Is My Song."

Does God Belong to Congress?

by Michael B. Walters

PURPOSE:

To help youth understand that God is not a member of any political party and that there are Christians of good conscience in all the major political parties in the United States.

PREPARATION

➡ Prepare the pole position signs. (See FYI, "Take a Stand.")

➡ Have the scavenger hunt items ready, including the several copies of the *Book of Discipline*.

➡ Have a Bible and a copy of *The United Methodist Hymnal* for each person and a commentary on Exodus.

➡ Provide newsprint and markers or chalk and a chalkboard.

FOR YOUR INFORMATION

POLITICAL CLAIMS: Topics for younger youth

* prayer in school
* public funding of private religious schools
* sex and AIDS education in schools
* gay rights
* regulating sex, violence, and profanity on TV or in the arts
* gun control
* immigration

POLITICAL CLAIMS AND GOD (5 minutes)

Older Youth

➡ Brainstorm answers to this question: What are some current issues for which politicians make the claim that God is on their side? List the responses on the chalkboard or newsprint. You will refer to this list several times.

Younger Youth

➡ Put up the "Political Claims" list. (See FYI.)

➡ Ask the participants to identify the issues that people are most likely to claim God's support for. Place an X next to each issue that participants feel falls into this category. List any other new issues the group mentions. You will refer to this list several times.

TAKE A STAND (5 minutes)

➠ Use the issues identified in the previous activity to do a pole position exercise. (See FYI.)

➠ Place the pole position signs in a line across the room. Explain that the group members are to take a firm stand on these issues by standing near the sign that most clearly indicates their position.

➠ Call out the listed issues and have participants take a stand. Ask the group members to observe where the most people and the least people stand. Discuss the reasons for the response.

MORALITY BY MAJORITY RULE (5-10 minutes)

➠ Assign **Exodus 23:2, 6-9.** Give the participants a chance to research this passage in the commentary. Then discuss the following questions. (See FYI.)

> In a democracy, majority rules. In light of the Scripture, is the majority always right? Give a reason for your answer.
> Do you think this principle applies to small groups such as churches and youth groups as well as to countries? Why, or why not?
> How do you think people (or groups) try to get others to agree with their beliefs?

TAKE A STAND

"Pole Positions" is a forced ranking game. Make numbered signs from 1 to 10. Number 10 is "very strongly agree" and number 1 is "very strongly disagree." Post these signs in a horizontal line around the room. When you read aloud the statement, the group members will stand near the number that best illustrates their level of agreement.

This game helps youth discover the values they already have, and helps them see the diversity within their own group. If, however, everyone agrees on one position, you can use the opportunity to talk about why, or you can suggest different slants or viewpoints on the issue that may not have occurred to anyone and then ask the participants to change positions according to new insights. Seek out reasons for and values behind the diversity of opinion and mention new ways of looking at an issue when there is a great similarity of opinion.

MORALITY BY MAJORITY RULE

This brief passage can be expanded to include other verses that highlight justice issues. The main questions are, "Does popularity make an issue right or wrong?" "Does what is best or most desirable for the many justify not meeting the needs of the few?"

"WHERE IS THE CHURCH?" SCAVENGER HUNT

Participants are to search the church for the following:

1. the page and paragraph number of the *Discipline* where you find the official United Methodist stance on abortion, divorce, human sexuality, rights of youth and young adults
2. title and page number of a hymn about justice or social concerns
3. six of the eight basic freedoms the Social Principles claims all governments must allow
4. the page number of a hymn about letting peace begin with me on earth
5. a political symbol in most churches
6. a religious statement written on government property
7. a picture of someone doing something spiritual that a public school teacher can not force someone to do
8. something political in a church newsletter or bulletin

Suggested scavenger hunt "finds"

1. abortion (Par. 71G); divorce (Par. 71D); human sexuality (Par. 71F); rights of youth and young adults (Par. 72D)
2. See the index of the *Hymnal*, pages 946 and 952.
3. See the *Discipline*, Par. 74A.
4. hymn 431
5. the American Flag, the Roll of Honored Veterans
6. "In God We Trust" on money
7. prayer, Bible reading
8. 4th of July Picnic, Flag Day observance, political rally, petition of letters to send to elected officials

INFOMERCIAL (15 minutes)

Older Youth

➡ Choose one to three issues from the earlier exercise on which the group was the most divided.

➡ Form two to six teams, according to their stand on the issue. Each team will act out its infomercial.

➡ Allow each team seven minutes to create an infomercial for an imaginary political candidate who takes the opposite side from the one they had originally agreed on. Remind the participants to make claims that show how God is on their side. (For example, one team is pro-choice on abortion and creates a campaign for a pro-life position.)

➡ After the presentations, discuss any changes, reaffirmations, discoveries, or insights gained.

Younger Youth

➡ Choose two or three issues on which the group was fairly divided.

➡ Form opposing debate teams and designate a moderator.

➡ Allow each team seven minutes to create an argument for the position opposite to the one they really hold (as the older youth did for the infomercial).

➡ The moderator will lead a debate in the style of a TV news show. Debaters can read their responses or use them as notes, adding other comments.